MW00849129

PRAISE FOR THE BOOK

> Don't risk fading into the SE background. Read this book and learn how easy and liberating it can be to be a Social SE!

BOB RIEFSTAHL, AUTHOR OF *DEMONSTRATING TO WIN!*

> Patrick sends a clear message to all SEs: DARE TO CREATE!

STEFFEN MÜLLER, PATHFINDER CONSULTING

> Really enjoyed the innovative approach and the lessons within the story. I'll be using these into my own posts and efforts.

GREG HOLMES, THE SALES ENGINEER GUY

> A great insight to Sales Engineering and the nuances of a great role and career choice.

SEMIR JAHIC, CLARI

Entertaining mix of Elias Story to the frontline of Thought Leadership combined with Timeless principles for Social Content. A must for every modern Solution Engineer. If you think you knew everything, this book will proof you wrong!

PHILIPP SCHÖNE, SE LEADER, MULESOFT

Genuinely amazing.

EDWARDO S. RIVERA, GM SECTEC

Engaging, inspiring, vivid and thought provoking. Patrick manages to take the reader on a journey through a difficult topic in a way that really empowers the reader to take action and the first step towards thought leadership.

ELIAS FREITAG, SENIOR MANAGER SOLUTION ENGINEERING, SALESFORCE

If you're in technical sales – or in any field for that matter – and aspire to become viewed as a thought leader in your industry, this book is for you. In unique fashion, Patrick masterfully takes the reader on a journey through the eyes of Elias – a young sales engineer trying to find his voice and navigate his way to prominence. Learn timeless principles of how to elevate your own, personal brand as you follow Elias through the trials and tribulations of dealing with customers, sales, and marketing, and the delicate politics of putting oneself out there.

CHRIS WHITE, AUTHOR OF *THE SIX HABITS OF HIGHLY EFFECTIVE SALES ENGINEERS*

THE SOCIAL SALES ENGINEER

THE SOCIAL SALES ENGINEER

TIMELESS PRINCIPLES FOR ACHIEVING THOUGHT
LEADERSHIP

PATRICK PISSANG

Foreword by
DON CARMICHAEL

// 1. Auflage 2021 (1.0.0)
// Copyright © 2021 Patrick Pissang
// All rights reserved.
// Website: https://saleshero.training

// Editor: Ameesha Green www.thebookshelf.ltd
// Proofreading: Florian Führen
// Cover Design: George Stevens www.gsharpmajor.com

// Thanks to the Beta Readers: Don, Bob, Chris, Greg, Steffen, Semir, Philipp, Mohamed, Damian, Elias, Edwardo, Michael, Melanie

// ISBN Paperback: 978-3-9822147-7-1
// ISBN Hardcover: 978-3-9822147-8-8
// Buch erschienen bei: ZEMP Golden Goose GmbH, Salachweg 18a, 86807 Buchloe, Bayern
// Das Werk, einschließlich seiner Teile, ist urheberrechtlich geschützt. Jede Verwertung ist ohne Zustimmung des Verlages und des Autors unzulässig. Dies gilt insbesondere für die elektronische oder sonstige Vervielfältigung, Übersetzung, Verbreitung und öffentliche Zugänglichmachung.

Bibliografische Information der Deutschen Nationalbibliothek
Die Deutsche Nationalbibliothek verzeichnet diese Publikation in der Deutschen Nationalbibliografie; detaillierte bibliografische Daten sind im Internet über http://dnb.dnb.de abrufbar.

Please leave a review on Amazon or Goodreads! For a better Karma.

For all my dear friends, students, and mentors in the secret kingdom of sales engineering!

CONTENTS

1

FOREWORD

FOR SALES ENGINEER (SE) PROFESSIONALS, business social tools and the skills needed to master them are now near the top of our enablement to-do list. In addition, influencing and establishing credibility at scale is now a fundamental part of the SE role.

In my sales engineer skills workshops, I meet many seriously skilled technologists who are perfectly capable presenters and communicators but are completely 'tongue-tied' when it comes to social media. It's usually a combination of fear of breaking their employer's social media rules and a lack of confidence in their 'voice', imagining they have nothing to say or that no one will want to engage with their content. Or sometimes, there's a cultural barrier; some countries value privacy to the point that they feel uncomfortable posting anything online. In 2020, I met a skilled and articulate SE specialist experimenting with blogging. The blog was brilliant—it was thought-provoking and showed thought leadership. They just needed help, coaching, and encouragement to evolve into a social influencer. Now that person has definitely mastered business social networks; they have a loyal and appreciative following—in fact, I regularly share their brilliant articles. Additionally, they host podcasts and are themselves invited onto other sales engineering influencers' podcasts and webinars.

We live in a 'social' world.

Humans are, of course, at their core, social creatures, but the digital 'social network' we've created far surpasses anything we were capable of before. Our digital social tools may still be very new—Facebook, for example, only launched in 2004. But as we look back, many historians will say they are as revolutionary as the invention of writing itself[1].

Perhaps surprisingly, LinkedIn, currently the preeminent professional networking platform, was launched the year before Facebook, in 2003. Still, it took a lot longer to grow to its current 756 million users across two hundred countries.

For many years, LinkedIn was viewed as little more than an online resume or a CV. Yet, even today, three people are hired through it every minute. Of course, LinkedIn is still a mighty job seeking and advertising tool, but its real power is now in professional influencing, building personal branding and credibility, showcasing expertise, and attracting new business connections.

This book is aimed at sales engineers who also go by many other names: PreSales Consultants, Sales Consultants, Cloud Architects, Solution Engineers, Customer Advisors are common role titles, but there are many, many more.

What connects all these roles is that they are primarily client-facing Business-to-Business (B2B) relationship. They form technical and business expert roles (industry, domain, and value) that employ advanced people with communication skills, commercial acumen, sales skills, passion, agility, an innovative mindset, and a fixation with lifelong learning.

If a fundamental part of the SE role is influencing and projecting technical and business authority and credibility, then the message is clear; whether it's influencing hidden buyers or hidden decision-makers, professional social network mastery is crucial.

As consumer buying behaviors leak into the business world, we're seeing some strong behavioral changes in how B2B tech buyers act.

They are now spending a significant portion (maybe two-thirds) of the buying process hidden from our sales colleagues, doing self-research, watching videos, consulting with their networks, and checking out video and other content on LinkedIn. Even when they engage in a sales process with us ('tripping the sales trip-wire'), some of the decision-makers remain hidden only to be accessed by internal champions who are willing to forward if we're lucky on our video, thought leadership, and influencing pieces.

Let Patrick's book guide you on your journey from treating business social networks as an online resume or a CV to realizing their true value in establishing credibility through social mastery and helping you evolve into a social influencer and thought leader.

—Don Carmichael
Chief PreSales Guru of Winning Skills Ltd.
August 31st, 2021

2

INTRODUCTION, OR HOW TO PUT WOOD INTO THE OVEN

"Social media is embarrassing!" you say. "I don't want to be part of the self-presentation business. Most of the stuff out there's irrelevant, out of context, and useless." You swipe your thoughts to the side with your hand.

But wait a second; isn't that a pretty superficial answer? Look at great movies, for example. Every fantastic story features a hero with external and internal problems. Tom Hanks's external challenges in *Cast Away* might have been to survive the years on the pacific island after his plane crash. But having achieved that, his life becomes even worse because his only love married somebody else. To eventually succeed, he had to overcome the internal problem of controlling and planning every aspect of his life.

So you don't like social media. This is your external problem.

But what about the internal one that fuels it? Could it also be true that you fear to put yourself out there? Could that be the real reason for your resistance; deep down in your heart, you want to express and share your thoughts?

If this resonates with you, then the book in your hands was

written for you. It's your toolbox for an approach to social media that gives you both a mental and practical framework.

Let this book be your stoic guide to overcoming your resistance. Let it hint you towards thought leadership without big fanfares and bland motivational phrases.

You aren't a flash in the pan, and the same should go for your brand.

Why should you bother reading this book?

There are many reasons for becoming a thought leader. Viewed from a distance, most of them may well be ego-based: fame, reputation, followers, daily praise, and a feeling of status and belonging. Thought leaders are influencers, and so money might be part of the equation, too.

If your motives are based on petting your ego, think twice before deciding to walk the thought leader's path. Those goals are external and not under your control, much like Tom Hanks' attempt to control time in *Cast Away*.

Don't ask yourself how you can become famous but rather how to cure the desire to be celebrated. That sounds philosophical because it is. If there's an inner resistance that wants to keep you at arm's length with your online presence, then ignore it. What could be wrong with sharing knowledge? Well, consciously or unconsciously, you already know the answer: it's a journey into an area that's psychologically and cognitively uncomfortable! The big reason to go for it anyway is that such endeavors are always the most rewarding. You should know that learning such a demanding new skill means a neuronal firework going off, making you feel more alive[1].

So, what motivates you?

We humans would be more easily convinced if we could experience the results before investing time in a new project. Our desire for instant gratification often sabotages our long-term goals[2]. By understanding our inner workings, we can push through negative thoughts.

There's a story about a rich guy who hiked in the mountains, lost his path, and spent the cold winter night alone. As he hadn't watched the weather forecast, he was surprised by a blizzard.

Life, in general, was favorable to that person, and he found an old hut. Freezing, he closed all the windows and doors. But although he could shut out the blizzard, he couldn't shut out the frost.

What kind of person was the lucky man in the hut? He was born into an affluent and peaceful society. He had won in the genetic lottery, business success seemed to come effortlessly, and he married an adorable spouse. He was richly gifted by life.

His shelter also contained a stove. But there was no wood left for a fire in this empty hut. It seemed whoever lived here before had burned everything.

Suddenly, the oven spoke to the lucky guy. "Fire me up, and I will warm you."

Surprised, he answered, "How am I supposed to do that?"

"Get out there and collect some wood."

The guy froze and didn't want to go out again to find firewood. He wasn't used to giving first; he demanded immediate results.

"What? If you are an oven, warm me up first. Prove that you can do it, and I will collect wood."

The lucky guy would be the only person who ever saw a puzzled oven. "That's not how I work."

"I don't care! I won't change my life's principles for a stupid oven."

That night the man lost his index fingers, and nearly his life, to the frost.

People seem to expect life to treat them well, to hand them their desired results before they are required to act.

Don't be that person. Don't expect the benefits of success before you take action. It's okay to feel intimidated because this is the reason why most people will never travel the route you are considering—the reason you are reading this book.

Leave your cozy seat, go out into the dark forest, sharpen your axe, cut down trees, chop them into pieces, and fire up the oven. You can be sure it will warm you.

All of those actions are under your control, no one else's. Start your thought leadership journey with this book. It'll tell you what you need to know and will motivate and mentally support you.

About the book

Do you know a tool for success that works while you sleep? Well, yes, one answer could be money. But you can employ a far more powerful tool called familiarity. If you bought this book, you are most likely selling enterprise software as a Sales Engineer, Account Executive, or Customer Success Consultant. When you look back at your career, has a prospect on a discovery call ever told you they had the feeling they wanted to know you? If yes, you've already tasted the power of being an industry VIP. If not, you aren't pulling all levers to simplify your life.

With this book, you will set the stage for your thought leadership journey, building a following, and maybe even gaining die-hard fans.

What if you could watch a series on your favorite streaming platform that told you the principles of how to become a thought leader? You wouldn't need to go to any courses, or even leave your sofa. This book takes our hero—a completely mediocre guy called Elias—on such a journey. In the next chapter, we'll dive into Elias' life as he struggles in his stalling career as a Sales Engineer.

Every chapter is followed by a timeless principle to inspire you. You are taking the steps into building your brand and making the world aware of your greatness.

Who will benefit from the book?

Essentially, everybody who is starting out on social media, tried but gave up, or uses it without much success. Those looking to leverage social media beyond using it as merely a resume or connection tool will greatly benefit.

Maybe you struggle to understand what this *beyond* could be for you. If so, this book will inspire you and provide you with digestible thinking tools. It's written with the least amount of words possible but with as many as needed. The chapters are short and quick to read. But make sure to digest them properly.

Always have a text marker handy as you read. Don't be shy with the book.

Remember to return to it too. Some lessons are beneficial when you start out, most likely those about mental models. Others become beneficial once you've been in the game for a while (how to write and edit your posts, for example).

As a beta reader put it, "The struggle is real, and it's worth the effort."

Your task is to find your singular voice and be genuine when building a social influencer brand. The book will be your essential guide.

—Patrick Pissang
Buchloe, Germany
September 3rd, 2021

3

THE ORDINARY LIFE OF A SALES ENGINEER

'HE WHO KNOWS EVERYTHING, FORGIVES EVERYTHING,' Herbert's newest post read. The text blurred in front of Elias' eyes. He shook his head in disbelief. How could his colleague dare to write such pseudo-wisdom? If he insisted on posting stuff, Herbert should stick to sales engineering.

He wouldn't write such nonsense if his parents had abandoned him as a child.

Angry, Elias clicked the comment icon and wrote, 'Herbert, stick with the things you know. ConnectedOut is a business platform, not a self-help one.'

The mouse hovered over the submit button as tears suddenly rolled down his cheeks. He could barely see anything. He pushed the laptop aside and sunk into the sofa. He was alone, as usual. And this was one of the times where he wished his grandparents were still alive. Nothing was important anymore; not Herbert, not sadness, not climate change, and not the client meeting tomorrow morning.

Elias fell asleep while the pillow absorbed his tears.

THE NEXT MORNING, Elias sat in his home office and stared at his laptop's clock. Only two more minutes, and he would join the discovery call. Well, it was more a demonstration of the solution than actually asking questions that mattered for the deal. Luckily, playing the role of an inquisitor wasn't enjoyable for him.

He never joined web meetings early because he feared that talking to the prospect would be necessary. In his world, the account executive had to build relationships. Elias never really knew what to say, and staying silent seemed to increase his credibility.

To bridge the minute before hitting the meeting's join button, he opened his social network ConnectedOut and invited Suzan, a Lead Architect. He'd met her during the demo he gave an hour ago. Posting or commenting online was not his style, but he invited all acquaintances from his business meetings to join his list. Occasionally, he would like other people's posts. The lead architect would be follower number two hundred.

Do I have to open a bottle of champagne and cheer myself now? Elias didn't get why people were trying to push that number as high as they could. It seemed Herbert followed that strategy with his posts. Agreed, they were sometimes entertaining, but they weren't worth a like from him. Social media was a dangerous game full of fluffy, empty sentences. But Elias recognized the braveness of Herbert putting himself out there.

While scrolling through his feed, a quote caught his eye: "If a man knows not to which port he sails, no wind will be favorable." The philosopher who said that was called Seneca and died two thousand years ago. A stoic.

Well, my winds blow in all directions, but I haven't reached any port. I am alone, and my career sucks. I could laugh more, enjoy my life more. Wow, that's the first quote that's made me actually think. What's up with me? Am I getting old?

Impressed by the quote, Elias updated his profile slogan.

Beneath his photograph now sat the title of Senior Sales Engineer and the statement "I love philosophy." Elias smiled, empowered by his spontaneity in overcoming his resistance to putting something personal out there.

Suddenly, his pulse hit hard in his veins. He was now two minutes late to the call. Due to his shaking hand, the mouse pointer missed the join button. Sighing, he concentrated and tried again. Waiting wheels were spinning, far too slow for his taste. By hammering his fingers on the table, he tried to speed up the dialing process. It didn't work.

Finally, three video feeds appeared. Elias saw his account executive Sarah speaking in the highlighted window. "I'm sure Elias will join soon. He's our feature database and our walking, talking documentation."

This description pumped up his ego, but it also offended a shadowy corner of his mind.

On the other screen, a bunch of people sat in a meeting room. They were too tiny to distinguish.

But they laughed at Sarah's comment. One of them said, "Well, maybe he has technical problems." The whole crowd chuckled.

Elias sweated because this was precisely the excuse he planned to use. "Hello, all. My other call went on longer than planned."

"What call?" Sarah asked, confused. She always scanned his calendar. "Anyway, great that you made it. I've already introduced us, and everyone is looking forward to watching your demo."

What an honor. Elias smiled mildly and nodded. "Okay then, let's go."

So he gave his usual Sellingpower software tour and replied confidently to the clients' questions. The prospect served Human Resources departments and wanted to use Sellingpower to streamline their sales processes. Very typical requirements for a typical client.

Once the nervousness of meeting new people was gone, Elias grew to the top of his game. Colleagues often asked him how he could lead a discussion while demoing. To answer this, he referred to the hero of his youth, Bruce Lee. *I don't fear a man who trains ten thousand kicks one time but the man who trains the same kick ten thousand times.*

As USUAL, the meeting went by quickly. Shortly afterward, Sarah called him. As she always did.

With a deep and proud voice, Elias answered the phone call. "Hi Sarah, how do you think it went?"

She didn't seem to be as enthusiastic as she normally was. "It went great, as always. You definitely are my one-night-demo-stand!"

"Will they sign?"

"You know, I love working with you."

"Is it because I was late?"

"No, it's not about the deal. What I wanted to say is that from now on, I'm going to be working for strategic accounts."

Elias gulped. The infamous strategic accounts. That meant he wouldn't partner with Sarah any longer. Only three people in the sales engineering team were entitled to work for them. Those boys and girls got the big commission checks and traveled to Mexico for the achievers club every year. Elias' personal social media hero, Herbert, was also part of that team.

Braggarts. Elias never understood what made those people special.

The last time he had seen Herbert—a so-called value architect—delivering a demonstration of their product to the team, it wasn't inspiring. There was no story, the flow was off, and he didn't know the software inside out. *And I thought Germans were the best engineers on the planet.* The way Herbert had spoken about the Sellingpower solution had bored Elias—it hadn't been technical enough for his taste.

"Okay. Well, congratulations on the promotion, Sarah."

"Thanks. By the way, your demo was great, and they will sign. It was good to work with you. I wish you could become a value architect."

Elias' throat tightened. "Well, no. It is not my style. Too salesy, I guess. That's not me."

"You could learn it. You have everything it takes. Just some practice in small talk and industry talk, and you're on your way."

I'm just not a people pleaser. "Clients want our technology, not me."

"Well, maybe you should give it a thought. All the best. I will miss working with you."

Sarah ended the call. Leaning back, Elias breathed out loudly. *What's her problem? I close nearly every opportunity for her if she gives me the chance to demo. What else does she want? Bigger deals? Is that it? I call that greediness.*

THOUGHT LEADERS FIND MEANING (IN PHILOSOPHY)

It's no coincidence that Seneca's wisdom[1] resonated with Elias. Whether they were winning or losing, the stoics stayed calm. They didn't freak out on significant achievements, and they didn't fall apart on failures.

Also, acceptance—the quality of not judging any situation as good or bad—isn't a sign of weakness but of greatness. It's not passive but an active step towards reality.

Most importantly, it can give your life purpose, namely to strive to become the best version of yourself. When opening up to the world on social media, this thought alone gives self-confidence.

Accepting that wins and losses are a part of life, a stoic thought leader would train and prepare for the bad times. Especially during calm and cozy periods when people seem to dislike artificial discomfort. Can you confront yourself a little with daily challenges? Fast for a day, sleep on the floor, pretend not to have a car, only use cold water, and so on? This »training for bad times« is a core of stoic philosophy and one of the main reasons why contemporaries labeled them pessimistic. Get up from the garden chair (or sun lounger if you prefer) to work on your skills, especially those that help prepare for downers.

Create a book full of ideas for bad days, build a network, and use affirmations to cope with critique. Once critique flows in—which is unavoidable; you can't control it—it will give you the necessary mindset.

In those traits lies all the mastery of yourself: preparation, daily routine, practice, and learning from mistakes. Accept that only your reasoned choice is what you control.

Every other situation you face is a judgment of your thoughts. You label it good or bad because an external event in itself is neutral. It doesn't care about you.

In that sense, stoics wouldn't muse about the number of post likes. The philosopher would think about how to please at least one person—if you can't make one fan happy, how can you possibly believe in managing one thousand or more? It's okay to set goals for likes, views, comments, and followers, but stay away from comparison. Be happy with your current state and enjoy your pace of progress.

If you feel unhappy, turn down your desire for more instead of burning out by pushing harder and harder. The quiet period might give you the space for a disruptive idea that levels up your game. The stoic says that if you want to be wealthy, reduce your desire to own a lot of trash.

Yes, strive for success. But accept how little you have under control. Treat every person who shows interest in you as a friend.

Yes, bring value to others, but don't become arrogant when you get pleasing messages. Don't let yourself be carried away by that.

On the flip side, this attitude will allow you complete peace of mind should you fail. But most likely, you won't; your stoic persistence will lead you towards success.

Have the end in mind, yes, but find your meaning in playing the game by enjoying growing new skills and getting to know interesting people.

INSTANT CHALLENGE!

Look for a quote online that resonates with you.

Publish it and give it your spin. What are your thoughts on it? Is it puzzling, inspiring, or even nonsense?

#salesengineers #quote #creativity

INOPPORTUNE OPPORTUNITIES
COME OFTEN

ELIAS SCANNED HIS FAVORITE BLOG, one about the earth's plastic pollution.

What's wrong with us? Fish starving to death because their stomach is full of the plastic waste wrapped around your stupid sandwich?

Elias was still deep in thought when his phone rang. It was Sarah. He hadn't heard from her for weeks. In the meantime, he had worked with other account executives very successfully. Now Sarah called him. Did she want to get her one-night-demo-stand boy back?

"Hi Sarah, how are you?" he asked slowly, reading the last lines of the blog article.

"Haven't you heard?"

"That we produce more plastic than ever and plan to shoot it into the universe? Can you believe that?"

Sarah went silent, and Elias sensed she was fighting confusion. Then she said, "Hasn't your manager told you that I need you for an emergency demo? The call is going on right now. You should have gotten my invite."

"Ah, I deleted it because it was Herbert's account, not mine."

"Okay, don't worry, but please join now. I will send it again. It is urgent and a big, big opportunity. Pleeeeease."

"But Sarah, I have this…" She hung up. "…RfP to finish. Crap."

What should he do? Dial in? He hadn't heard about the request before. Usually, his manager would have volunteered him. He knew nothing about the account. Pulling up the record in Sellingpower—their very own Customer Relationship Management system, which Elias sold—he found himself assigned to a strategic opportunity called PeopleLove. Alongside Herbert.

Now his heartbeat went up. Shouldn't there be an email going out informing him about the assignment? He was pretty late for the web meeting, and he suddenly felt responsible for the deal.

Why do other people always put me in such situations?

Sarah's updated invite appeared in his inbox. He clicked the dial-in link.

I know enough about our product to rescue this. It wouldn't be the first time.

Elias shone in the meeting. Although lacking context, he maneuvered the conversation smoothly through riffs of sales process configuration and software compliance. PeopleLove even questioned the technical core of the platform, but Elias had heard it all before and dispelled any doubts.

The meeting went on for over an hour.

Shortly after the last-minute demonstration, Elias joined a private call for a recap. Herbert spoke to Sarah. As he realized Elias was attending, he stopped mid-sentence and approached his deal savior. "Amazing how you turned this around, Elias. The demonstration of the integration to the chat tool? Man, that exceeded their expectation for this requirement."

Herbert was apparently very excited by Elias' display.

Or was he just being polite and happy that I saved his skinny butt? "Thanks, Herbert." Elias wondered how value architects sold Sellingpower at all. They delivered a standard presentation, and there was nothing impressive about those if one knew a bit about software and sales processes.

Herbert nodded and smiled. "Glad to have you on board, mate."

"What happened? Why was that so urgent?" Elias asked.

"Well, we messed up when we researched the attendees. We thought they would be from the sales organization, but as you saw, they were all administrators."

"And what's wrong with administrators?"

"It's often a waste of time talking to them. We are aiming for a strategic deal, and going too deep into technicalities isn't helpful at this stage."

Confused, Elias' mouth opened without making any noise. The thing he loved to show off had no value? The features he explained day in, day out to close a lot of deals with were worthless?

Elias couldn't hide the annoyance in his voice. "Well, this time at least, it seems it was worth something."

"Agreed. You saved us big-time. Maybe you can join our meetings in the future, too, so we always have a backup."

Elias didn't think he was the one to decide. "If management, I mean Ralf, agrees... Sure."

THOUGHT LEADERS WENT THROUGH THE THRESHOLD

ELIAS DOESN'T ENJOY CHANGE, much like every other human being. But he loves stories about normal people who become heroes. Because, there is an underlying concept in the outstanding books and movies of our time: the hero's journey[1]. It was first researched by Joseph Campbell[2], then his findings were adopted by Hollywood, especially by Christoph Vogler[3], who created a playbook for screenwriters and novelists to write compelling stories. Elias' story also follows Campbell's blueprint. Have a look for it online.

But let's take a look at a famous example: *Star Wars*, which is a prime example of a powerful, resonating version of the hero's journey. At some point early in the transformative story, our hero crossed a threshold, one with no possibility of return.

It happened when Luke Skywalker discovered that stormtroopers had killed his aunt and uncle. The Empire's actions reached him. Luke's best opportunity was to contact Obi-Wan Kenobi. He would go with him to Alderaan and learn to handle the force, despite this meaning that he would have no way back into his old life, just like his father before him.

From that point on, all actions drove the hero to success and to become someone else—someone greater than he ever dared to imagine. A thought leader should create a threshold: a situation or a message to the world that creates an irreversible decision.

Put yourself out there or make an internal decision that there's no way back. You decided to be a thought leader, an influencer, a hero in your industry, and that means, by definition, you will face opposition, derogatory comments, and envy. You will put people off; you may even be laughed at.

But having said that, a hero or heroine usually assembles a group of helpful allies around themselves. Your network will grow. People will want to support your mission as they feel compelled by leaders and visionaries.

Don't expect to become a thought leader by sticking to business-as-usual. If that were enough, you already would be where you want to be.

Make the conscious decision to become the person you dream about instead.

Bear in mind what Johann Wolfgang von Goethe once said: "Everybody wants to be somebody; nobody wants to grow."

What excuses does your mind come up with that you can't do it? Do you think you're not creative enough? Are there not enough hours in the day? Do you think you wouldn't have the stamina to stick with it? Do you lack writing skills? There are more reasons not to do it than you can possibly count, and they will hunt you down if you don't create your threshold, your point of no return.

INSTANT CHALLENGE!

Take a pencil and write on this page:

»I'm new here! From today on, you'll see me more often.«

Then take your smartphone's camera, zoom in, take a selfie, and publish it.

#salesengineers #iamhere #threshold

7

ME OR THE SHAMAN

FOUR WEEKS WENT BY, and Elias supported several meetings with the prospective strategic partner, PeopleLove. Sarah and Herbert seemed to only speak about abstract things. They asked questions that Elias thought were inquisitive: What happens if you don't solve your current problem? Why haven't you solved the problem before? How long have you had this issue? Why are you looking at Sellingpower at all? What impact would the solution have in your workplace? How would your competitors react?

Elias didn't get it. In his mind, the sales engineer should show a prospect the value of the product. Before that, the sales team shouldn't dare to ask questions. Was he missing the point?

That Wednesday morning, his laptop woke him from his daydream by playing the doodly meeting invitation sound. He was chilling out on his balcony, enjoying the morning sun, and sipping green tea. The invite was for Friday afternoon.

Oh crap, same time as our raid. When I don't show up again, my guild leader will replace me with this weird orc shaman. This guy has been after my core team slot for months and is just waiting for the opportunity to grab it.

Elias forced his mind back to work and inspected the invite. It was titled *Vision | Value | Viability*. The invite included the whole account team plus the VP of Sales, Ralf.

Suddenly, Elias' heart beat faster.

Alright, this meeting seems to be important. Who else is on there?

There were three PeopleLove employees Elias didn't know. That was weird; he had been consulting this company for over four weeks now and thought he would have heard all the stakeholders' names by now. The invite listed a woman called Jessica Da Bresco.

He was so curious about this seemingly important meeting that he searched for Jessica on ConnectedOut. She was easy to find. Her photograph showed a woman with a professional smile. Elias guessed that she was at the end of her thirties and the beginning of an impressive career. He scanned the rest of her profile. Like Ralf, she had the title of VP of Sales. Gulping, he thought, *This is what Sarah meant by moving up the ladder.*

His palms started sweating, and he felt his heart beating in his throat. *Oh man, now Jessica will see that I visited her profile. Should I invite her? What would she think when I did? What would she think if I left her profile without asking her to connect?*

He stared across the street where some lonely trees formed a measly park. Shame filled his breast and throat. *What am I so scared of? This isn't rational! Our planet is dying, and I'm afraid of a profile page?*

Still feeling uneasy, he closed the social media page, not having invited Jessica. Before entering his flat, he raised his chin towards the sun. Then he sighed and navigated towards his desk.

I better prepare a good demo for Friday.

For the first time in the last four weeks, Elias was happy that Herbert would also join the call. Without his colleague, he wouldn't feel confident demoing Sellingpower to a VP.

8

THOUGHT LEADERS DO THE UNEXPECTED

ELIAS IS CALLED to action on his hero's journey, but he ignores it. He prefers to stay a mediocre guy and preserve the status quo.

But you are wiser than our hero, right? You understand that if you want extraordinary results, you can't lead with mediocre approaches. Quite the opposite: you need to be above the ordinary in everything you do.

The easiest way to achieve the unexpected is by questioning the status quo. To do this, simply be lazy. Yes, be lazy!

Think about how you do sales engineering today. Just by looking at daily chores and how to avoid them, you will be presented with lots of ideas. You are required to do a demonstration; you are requested to perform a proof of concept, or you are assigned to answer RfPs. The tasks in themselves don't provide value. They are simply reflexes developed during thousands of sales cycles.

Now ask yourself, how can I be lazy and not do that stuff and still provide value?

Let's take the proof of concept. The lazy way of doing it is not to do it at all. Well, indeed, you will get into trouble getting that past your management. But maybe there's a more subtle way. What about having it done by somebody else, such as your prospect? Easy, isn't it?

But how would that add value and for whom?

The following answer is field-tested and has been practiced multiple times with complex enterprise application integration and API software: have the client do the PoC! Think this is impossible because it's too risky, your tool is too complex, it could rain, or you just prefer traditional approaches? Sometimes, we shouldn't believe every thought we think.

Let's just assume it could work and clients would implement the PoC. What's the value?

Firstly, it's entirely unexpected when you explain to your client that they will perform the PoC. If they have skin in the game—the deal—they will take the task. Of course, you will be virtually or physically assisting this timeboxed endeavor as a coach.

Secondly, it's crucial to follow a challenging goal and work on a strategic problem with the PoC. That way, the client team will get to know your tool and (partly) solve their strategic problem. They can see how it benefits their future daily life to purchase your solution.

Thirdly, the client team can demonstrate your solution internally by using their company's language. Such a presentation is the most effective way of doing a demo. And, ta-da, it doesn't involve effort on your end! The client's employees and members of their PoC team will be nervous and prepare diligently. Those kinds of demos are usually persuasive.

Having a client running their own PoC with untrained personnel on a spotlight project seemed inconceivable in the middleware industry. Results, though, were impressive once the client and the account team could be convinced to run a PoC the "lazy" way.

Thought leaders think about what seems impossible; they don't just reject contrary ideas outright. Follow your instincts and try what wasn't tried before. Failing allows learning, and your organization should support it.

INSTANT CHALLENGE!

Take a second to think about three unexpected moves you could make when meeting a client. They should still add value. Think of whether there is a different way to execute a workshop or to present in a new way.

Write down the three ideas here and highlight the best.

Do you dare to implement it?

#salesengineers #differentiation #unexpected

9

SILENCE MAKES THE RIGHT PEOPLE SPEAK

FRIDAY'S executive meeting came faster than Elias expected. Demo-wise, he was prepared as usual. He did a network speed test to ensure his line was working okay and then logged into the video call from home at the exact minute the meeting was scheduled to start.

Nervously, Elias scanned the participants' panel at the edge of his screen. There was Jessica, the VP of Sales. She didn't seem to have had the best morning. *Was she also kicked out of her guild? Stupid orc shaman guy. Those Germans take over my world. Has she realized that I visited her profile?*

The PeopleLove people still needed some time to organize themselves. Some joined, some left, and Jessica asked for patience. From the Sellingpower team, there were Sarah and Ralf, the VP of sales. Shocked by an observation, Elias scanned the participants' panel a second time.

Where is Herbert? Germans are never late!

The meeting should have started six minutes ago, and so Elias guessed something was wrong.

Suddenly, Sarah unmuted herself. "Sorry. I reached Herbert. He's ill, so he won't be joining us."

Elias closed his eyes as tears appeared in the wrinkles.

"I am sorry to hear that. Please send him my regards," Jessica said. "We're all set now."

Sweat flowed down Elias' back, and his shirt was sucking it up. It clung to his skin. He desperately tried to move his body to get it loose.

"Elias, are you going to take over from Herbert?" That was Ralf. He seemed pretty serious.

Still wrestling with his shirt, Elias answered, "Well, in this case, we might move the meeting because Herbert prepared all the information. I just had the demo part." As the words came out of his mouth, they sounded weak to him. *I'm such a sucker.*

"You have to unmute. We can't hear you," Sarah said.

Crap. Elias clicked the mic and kicked his weak side in the butt by saying, "Okay, yes. Of course, I will take over."

Oh, boy.

And he did. Headfirst into a meeting where he hadn't prepared anything but the demo. The latter just flowed; it came naturally. But Elias struggled to take over Herbert's role. Instead, he dug deep into technical aspects of the solution. The following thirty minutes went by like he was watching an immersive movie. Ralf and Sarah were talking excitedly with the PeopleLove team, but it sounded like white noise to Elias. A little later, he heard himself saying goodbye.

The meeting ended, leaving Elias with a weird feeling of incompleteness at having spoken about a topic nobody understood.

An hour later, the team regrouped without the prospect for an internal account review.

"Why didn't you say that you weren't prepared to run such a high-caliber session?" Ralf asked, trying to stay calm. His voice was breaking up as if he was coughing.

Elias knew he'd messed up. "I thought the demonstration would be good. How could I know they didn't want to take a look at the software?"

Ralf's voice pitched higher, and he spoke faster. "Really?

We're talking to executives! They don't care that our tool has AI as smart as Elon Musk. All they want to know is how it helps them print more money."

There was nothing more that Elias could say. He felt terrible; he felt terribly stupid.

Suddenly, he recognized his arrogance towards Herbert. His colleague spoke a different language to bridge the gap between technology and executive business parlance.

"Great. Now that you really should say something, you stay quiet." It seemed as if Ralf would never recover from this.

"Let's try to see this as an opportunity," Sarah said. "They will clearly remember us now. Herbert, Elias, and I will work on a comeback plan."

"Do you still want him on the team?" Ralf asked Sarah.

Silence.

Sarah?

Elias leaned closer to his laptop screen. His ego yelled very loudly, *Say yes, Sarah!* He hated the business game, but he hated the idea of being disliked even more. Colleagues would gossip about him when he left the team, and his career would be in danger if they took him off the account. People had been fired from Sellingpower for less.

Elias acknowledged his fault, and he planned to correct it. "I will do what is needed to turn things around," he finally said into the quietness.

Sarah smiled. "Silence always makes the right people speak."

It seemed like Ralf had calmed down. "Okay, Elias. Please learn how to become a trusted advisor. Study Herbert working with clients; shadow him as often as you can. Gosh, you should sleep in his bed if you can bear a guy in *schlafanzug*."

Elias nodded while he held his breath. He had no idea how this was achievable. Was he the right person for such a job? The product part came naturally to him, but the business aspects seemed tricky and detached from his interests.

There he'd gone, demoing along and potentially screwing up a big deal. But he didn't want to hide from his mistakes. "Thanks, Ralf and Sarah, for giving me this opportunity."

And thanks for throwing me into this crap in the first place. Not my fault!

10

THOUGHT LEADERS TALK ABOUT PROBLEM-SOLVING, NOT FEATURES

STOIC PHILOSOPHY SUGGESTS that you stop thinking that your problems are unique. Whatever happened to you today has happened to somebody else before. This perspective on life helps you relax in troublesome times and soothes your ego when praise is flooding in.

Thanks to Copernicus, humans started accepting that we aren't the center of the universe. And surely what's true for our solar system should be valid for life and business too.

When it comes to sales, not really. People cling to their problems because they love them; they need them. Problems let us grow and learn. They let us fall, giving us the chance to stand up again and continue our fight.

On your thought leadership journey, a problem has another function too. It allows you to distinguish yourself in your domain.

Category design[1] is the term for this concept. Elias can't become an influencer if he doesn't understand niches and thinks that leading with a solution isn't an inspiring sales approach.

He should learn instead to become problem-focused! In an optimistic way, of course.

Category design is the art of positioning, product development, customer focus, and culture building. Positioning theory suggests focusing on the core problems of a human, a society, or a business. So, when you brainstorm for your thought leadership domain, don't go into the nitty-gritty of an (ever-changing) process but convey a broader need.

For example, don't develop content on baking bread, but on living healthily with the right kind of bread.

There are examples of influencers in the tech realm who got successful quickly with posting admin how-tos for specific applications and vendors, but you need to understand that those topics have a half-life; they expire. Additionally, you depend on the vendor's success, adoption, and strategy. It might be worth thinking about writing content one or two levels higher. Think about which problem the application you would write how-tos for solves. Can you address the fundamental—maybe even timeless—need?

Once you've identified the basic need, you should give it a spin and frame it originally.

A prime example of a category design play is Salesforce[2]. During their early days, they created a new unknown problem. After decades, they still lead as the number-one solution provider to that self-created problem: storing customer data in maintenance-heavy, unreliable, and expensive data centers. By creating a cloud solution, they solved their very own problem. Brilliant.

The desire Salesforce touched was the need for sales teams to be both faster than the competition and hip. Isn't it clever to include a status aspect? Humans are very interested in their reputation. This way, Salesforce also cultivated a pop culture around technology.

Google reframed search on the web. You know the story, but are you aware that they framed a new problem? The common solutions during the early days got search completely wrong by crawling the web and building lists. Google's brilliant solution was to use backlinks as an indicator of quality. And with this, they fulfilled a basic need for marketers! They invented targeted ads. They taught marketers the unsolved problem of reaching a concrete buyer avatar on the web. Before Google, they would place apps on websites, no matter who visited them. Try to replicate that approach.

1. **Hunt for a domain you understand:** sales engineering.
2. **Identify a basic need:** sales engineers want to be acknowledged and not be seen as demo dollies.
3. **Define a problem for your audience:** sales engineers are labeled as techies and not perceived as valuable in the deal cycle.
4. **Be provocative about it by reframing the problem:** Advise sales engineers to become independent, lead each client with a vision, and qualify based on that.
5. **Then solve it with your content:** present use cases and examples. Creativity hacks. Success stories. Toolkit ebooks. Hold up a mirror.

Congratulations, you just created solutions by leading with a problem.

INSTANT CHALLENGE!

What's your category? Use the margin on this page to crystalize the ideas running through your brain right now.

Then, take a photo and publish it.

#salesengineers #positioning #category

11

A BEGGAR'S ADVICE DOESN'T COME CHEAP

THE FRUITY SMELL of freshly brewed tea surrounded Elias. He sat in his favorite teahouse, eating tiffin and enjoying the green walls, which made him feel welcome. The centuries-old armchair complained by squeaking when Elias leaned back after reading Herbert's latest social media post.

Elias tried to suck up every drop of knowledge his colleague dumped. The article provoked his interest, but technology didn't play a big part in it. Pressing the like button, the number below the post counted up to sixty seven. Then Elias investigated who also appreciated the article. A popup window listing the other sixty six people opened up. Elias didn't know most of them, but what stood out were their titles: Director, VP, CEO, or Founder.

His fingers massaged his temples. Suddenly, he raised his head and shouted, "I will never be able to do this!" Drops of spittle landed on his display. Then he ducked and checked whether anybody had heard his outburst.

No reaction from other guests, only from his voice within. *I don't want to end up like my parents. No, not that thought again! Not here. But what would my colleagues say if I started posting stuff like this? They would laugh at me.*

Carefully, he wiped the laptop with the corner of his shirt.

Where is the value in replicating Herbert? There are no topics I could write about. I'm not unique, and I don't want the spotlight.

With both hands, Elias covered his face. Warm tears ran through his fingers and down his cheeks. He hated crying because it reminded him of the time his parents left him. For weeks, he had cried. He thought he would dry out, and then things would be over. A painful knot in his stomach brought back the soul-crushing childhood emotions.

After a while—Elias couldn't say how long—a *beep-beep* from his laptop woke him up. He didn't recognize the sound.

Was there some hidden application running? A virus?

Elias studied the open browser tabs. One of them showed the symbol of a speaker. It was ConnectedOut. Had he received a message there? That happened so rarely he couldn't even remember any of the conversations.

Nervously, Elias clicked the tab into focus and checked the inbox. There was an unread message from Jessica Da Bresco. She had participated in the meeting when Elias messed up; the day Herbert was ill. Thinking out loud, he murmured, "The PeopleLove VP. Why is she contacting me? Is it to yell at me because I wasted their time?"

The attentive waitress thought Elias was talking to her. "Do you want another cup?"

He nodded and shyly smiled.

"Of course, just a second," she said.

Red-faced, Elias looked down at his display again. Without opening the direct message, he could read the preview. 'Hi Elias, Armor…'

Is this a fake account sending spam? His mouse pointer hovered over the read more button and then jumped to the delete button. *Not to open it would be the best thing to do, wouldn't it? This social media stuff is dangerous; what if, what if…*

He ended up pressing neither button. Giving in to his

unease, he closed the laptop, stood up, and went for a very early dinner.

We are all offspring of the most cowardly individuals from the stone age. Running away is so deeply ingrained in us.

"Please, cancel my tea," he said to the waitress, giving a generous tip. She didn't seem to care too much and waved him goodbye.

Walking to his favorite Indian lunch place, he thought about his next steps. The promise he gave Ralf and Sarah clung like a weight attached to his feet.

How on earth should I correct my mistake? He had no idea at all.

After reaching the restaurant district, the smell of food made him forget his troubles for a moment. Suddenly, he thought about potential articles to publish. Should he merge Indian food with his job and make something interesting from the juncture for a post? Was rice like the core data in the Sellingpower CRM? It didn't taste all that interesting before you mixed it with Mandala sauce. But how did this connect to the real world? Elias shook his head. Like a light spot in his eyes, Ralf's demand still burned in Elia's mind.

Okay, Elias. Please learn how to become a trusted advisor. Study Herbert working with clients; shadow him as often as you can. Gosh, you should sleep in his bed if you can bear a guy in schlafanzug.

It had been his worst idea to assume he could make up for his mistake by becoming someone else—a person with talents he didn't possess.

He had run away from so many things in his life.

Why didn't I run when Ralf yelled at me? This ridiculous situation will end my career at Sellingpower. I am so stupid.

Passing by a streetlamp, he hit it hard with his fist. Pain flooded his whole body. Elias grimaced and shook his hurting fingers.

Crap, am I a magnet for silly ideas?

A homeless person who sat two meters down the street had

been watching him. With a serious look, he asked, "What's up, mate?"

Surprised, Elias looked at the guy. He could only have been in his thirties. He was sat on some newspapers, holding up a sign that said, 'Got fired for being me.'

Shaking his shoulders, Elias told the man what was on his mind. "I'll tell Ralf that I'm not going to do it. If he fires me, so be it. But it doesn't make sense. I'm just not the right person."

"Sounds like you're running away." The man revealed his yellow teeth in a smile.

"And?"

"Usually, there's a way to succeed."

Elias was puzzled. "What?"

"Look, you're afraid of failing. But people often forget that they have the freedom to shape a situation so that it fits their strengths."

"What does that have to do with me?"

"You're not differentiating yourself. You are utterly normal, right?"

"Man, what's up with you?"

"What would your colleagues say if I asked them to describe you?"

Elias stood there, stunned. His eyes wandered to the sky, his mouth opened, ready to release the answer, but nothing came.

"You're running away from a task that jumped out of another person's mind, correct?"

"You live on the street and apparently lost your job because you were 'different.'" Elias pointed to the beggar's sign. "Why should I listen to you?"

"Better you didn't." The man's smile made Elias look away. "Do you have some change?"

Elias rummaged in his pocket and gave the guy a generous amount.

"Thanks, mate."

Suddenly, Elias felt much better and left the guy alone. It helped to help.

Maybe he is right? Maybe I could find differences between Sellingpower and a typical CRM. I know that stuff. Crazy ideas are my specialty.

A smile reached his mouth and then his eyes. Some minutes later, he enjoyed an outstanding mix of rice and sauce—business-analogy-free butter chicken.

12

THOUGHT LEADERS ENVISION (THEIR) FUTURE

DOES Elias lack a vision of who he wants to be? Or does he let life and its random events drive him? Thought leaders not only paint a compelling vision for their industry, awakening a desire in people to build a different future now, but they also envision *their* destiny and what sets them apart. Some create a vision board with pictures and quotes indicating how they will live, how they will be perceived, the number of followers they will accumulate, or how they will perform on stage in front of thousands of people. (Remember though, don't use this number for comparisons with others but for goal setting. If you compete, then compete with your future self by thriving to improve daily.)

But there's more: thought leaders plan their week, every week. They plan content, grow their idea journal, and execute the most critical routine: work on their brand positioning daily.

What is brand positioning, and how can you leverage it? It's the concrete definition of who you are and how you differ from the rest of the crowd. There's a straightforward positioning framework that you can employ to formulate such a vision of yourself. It's built on six pillars:

1. **Be different, not better.**
2. **Be exceptional.**
3. **Be the first.**
4. **If you can't be the first, create a category.**
5. **Target a niche, not a wide range of topics.**
6. **Fulfill a basic need.**

Let's get concrete with an example and assume you sell a Customer Relationship Management (CRM) application with AI components. You want to position yourself as the thought leader of AI in sales processes. The positioning framework helps you to find your spot.

1. **Be different, not better:** There might be other sales Engineers working in your domain. Most likely, they focus on the technical or administrative side of things. To differentiate yourself, you could consider the people aspect instead. Start telling stories and highlight how companies could introduce and leverage AI, or share how you've managed to make teams feel comfortable using AI. Don't try to outsmart everyone else by learning the newest technical framework's features. Winning such a battle is draining, and you will always lag behind. Find a new or underrepresented perspective, and think about it every day.

2. **Be exceptional:** Bring yourself on stage with unique content or approaches to reach your audience. Do you have more profound insights into a specific aspect of your domain that nobody else seems to be investigating? Is it weird? Perfect! You could publish your thoughts as a theme, for example: 'Why Technology Alone is Not Enough to Make Your Customers Successful.' If everyone relies on text posts, you have to start going live on your platforms

or sharing videos. Stand out and be memorable by sharing a provocative opinion and using different tools.

3. **Be the first:** If you can, be the first to climb the highest mountain or cross the Atlantic in an airplane. History will remember you. Of course, not everyone can be the first on Mount Everest, but technology offers many opportunities to be the first if you manage to discover an unsolved problem or master one that was thought to be impossible to solve. In the same way, you, as a thought leader, can invent or evangelize an approach that's novel in your industry.

4. **If you can't be the first, create a category:** Reinhold Messner wasn't the first person to beat Mount Everest, but people know him because he has climbed it first without a breathing aid. Carve out a new category from a larger one; specialize. Human-AI interaction could work in our fictitious case.

5. **Target a niche, not a wide range of topics:** Start small. AI and CRM are vast areas of content. Try to get into a specific aspect—lead qualification with account development teams using AI might be one of them.

6. **Fulfill a basic need:** This is undoubtedly the toughest one because it needs some levels of abstraction and experience. The point is, if you focus too much on processes (or technologies for that matter), you are vulnerable to changes. Instead, try to find a basic need and solve that: more deals, better qualifications, happier sales, cleaner customer records.

Think this framework through as often as possible. Read about positioning and marketing. Make a conscious effort to understand how audiences react and what attracts them.

INSTANT CHALLENGE!

Fill out a positioning framework for yourself or your organization in the empty space below.

Once you've finished it, publish a photo of it online.

#salesengineers #differentiation #positioning

13

WHAT YOU FEAR IS FEAR ITSELF

YODA'S LIGHTSABER glowed from the sideboard. Elias darkened the room because it matched his mood and his expectation of the coming conversation. As usual, he joined the web meeting that Ralf had set up for them on the dot. But he found himself parked in the lobby. The plan was to tell Ralf immediately that he had made a mistake and wanted to continue his preferred way of working: firing off demos like bullets from a machine gun.

Why do I suddenly think in war terms? Maybe because I miss playing video games? I haven't spent much time doing that lately — definitely a sign of too much work. I still haven't completed The Witcher. *Okay, man, concentrate.*

It seemed like his VP of Sales was stuck in an ongoing conversation. Elias inspected the interface of the conference tool, disabled his video, and muted himself. Then he switched the camera on again, checking his hair by observing his live picture.

Still, Ralf kept him waiting.

Beep-beep.

There was that sound again. Immediately, Elias remembered Jessica Da Brescos' message that he'd never read. He switched to his browser and scanned the social media inbox. She'd written again. Elias moved the pointer over the letter symbol and drew some circles around it.

Why does she care about me, writing me direct messages? Did I upset her?

He was still waiting for Ralf to start the call, so he used the time to check what Jessica had to say. A soft *click* reached his ear, and the messages opened.

Elias read the first one. Alongside a connection request, she wrote: 'Hi Elias, Amor Fati. Jessica.'

Puzzled, he looked at the cryptic message.

Was she mixing me up with somebody else? Maybe not. She used my name.

Nevertheless, he accepted the invitation to connect. Now curious, he read the second message. 'You remind me of me when I started in sales. Don't give up. I want to see you at the next meeting. Your ideas and concepts are valuable. Don't forget, it's not the situations that are good or bad; it's how you judge them. All the best, Jessica.'

"What the...?" Elias looked around as if he expected to see someone watching him. Her messages sounded more than strange to him. They were almost mystical.

Amor Fati. It's not the situation. Don't give up.

His daydream fell apart once he heard a man's voice.

"Hey Elias, thanks for waiting. The forecast call ran over." It was Ralf, waking him up. Elias abruptly closed his browser and straightened his spine. Smiling, he looked at the VP of Sales.

"Hi Ralf, no worries. Thanks for finding a slot for me."

"No problem—although you have only fifteen minutes now. I'm back to back."

Of course, it's my fault that his majesty overran. "Okay, I asked for this meeting because ..." Elias went silent.

Crap. Jessica weakened my conviction.

He wanted to cancel his strategic engagements, but now a

stranger was telling him to continue on his path. His opinion was suddenly wobbly, like a Jenga tower.

No, I can't take back the promise I made. I would look like a coward.

"Where are you? Looks like you're sitting in a cave," Ralf said.

Elias cleared his throat and looked over to the Yoda figurine. "Yeah, something like that." Then he lowered his voice to sound more confident. "Well then, I'll keep it brief. I'm planning to post articles regularly about the CRM industry. You know, things like 'Sellingpower consultants are not the same as CRM consultants.' I wanted your blessing as this isn't what we Sales Engineers typically do."

Silence.

Ralf regarded Elias via the screen. "Sure, why not? Hand over your drafts to marketing, and speak with Maria."

"Will do."

"Was that it?"

"I think so." *Your highness.*

Ralf waved his hand, smiled mildly, and ended the meeting.

Elias stood up, opened the roller blind, and blinked into the sun.

Okay, let's face the situation. It's neither good nor bad—it's what I judge it to be. Challenge accepted!

14

THOUGHTS AGAINST YOUR ONLINE PRESENCE AS A THOUGHT LEADER

ELIAS MIGHT HAVE GIVEN up if it hadn't been for Jessica. Other people have the power to distract us from those nagging negative thoughts, but not everybody has such a person on hand. This book wants to take that role for a moment.

There you are, aiming to become a social media star known for your precious thoughts. And that's great, but you might come up against some barriers.

Do you know what an accusation audit[1] is? It's when you admit your faults before firing off your arguments or requests. The goal is to soothe the other party's emotions by addressing them early.

For example, you might have caused delay or friction in some deal because you couldn't answer a roadblock compliance question. When speaking to the client again, you would first do an accusation audit and list what could have been perceived negatively. Note, this is not an excuse for promises you missed to deliver—quite the opposite. Once you've delivered an accusation audit, you have to follow up with excellent work: "We got the impression that our pricing didn't meet your expectations. Please allow us to prove our value today."

Psychologically, this weakens the other party's concerns. So, let's do an accusation audit. Name the most likely setbacks you will have to deal with during your journey.

Here we go:

Have you ever realized that it's tougher to run a presentation or demo in front of colleagues than it is with clients? Why? You should feel safe in your company's environment, right? But it seems like co-workers are your most critical challengers. On that note, your colleagues might be wondering what you're suddenly doing online. Why do you publish your ideas so often? Do you want to impress somebody? Or are you fishing for a promotion? Be prepared to get that kind of feedback, then ignore it.

One evening, you might be lying in bed contemplating and realize that this social media stuff costs you an hour of work every day—valuable time you could have invested in compliance training or answering the RfP. You don't have the time to continue building your brand, or so you believe.

Don't believe every thought that randomly runs through your brain. Instead, build up a positive framework. You face a phase of instability to reach a new level—and yes, instability means less effectiveness, but not forever. Keep pushing, and things will get easier. Consider the typical hero who hits rock bottom only to be reborn with the new skills needed.

One of the biggest hurdles to overcome is a lack of vision. Or, to put it another way, you can't fully imagine your new hobby's effect on your career if results haven't yet materialized. The way to overcome this hurdle is to act as if they have.

A proven way of achieving your vision is to write about it every day. Documenting thoughts and ideas crystallizes them, and when you do this daily, you inevitably come to a state where your vision resonates so strongly with you that it pushes you forward. You become unstoppable.

Another hurdle may be compliance with your company's social media guidelines, which may appear complex and even frightening; you might fear harming the company or your colleagues. A recommended way forward is to be open with leaders and the marketing department about your plans. Get them on your side, explain the benefits of being visible and supporting the company's business. Or to do the complete opposite: separate your social media message from your work.

Maybe modesty once was a popular trait, but current research shows that it harms your perceived competency[2]. Being positive and confident even if you fail is better perceived than playing it humbly. So if you're not sure whether bragging puts off prospects and clients, then rest assured it doesn't. As is true for most things: the quantity makes the poison. These days, bragging on social media, for example, is accepted and even expected. "Humility is admirable. But if someone requests information or an answer that requires you to reveal positives about yourself, you should oblige."[3] Just look at the attention a job change, promotion, or course badge receives.

Another pushback that may arise from within is your ego. We all want to be acknowledged, but it's natural to be unsure of how our content will resonate when we begin this journey. You might be scared of people's judgments of your artistic endeavor. Unfortunately, there's no way around this other than to put your thoughts in front of an audience—even a critical or disinterested one. It hurts sometimes, and it should because that means you're growing. Make sure you learn from feedback, and please resist the urge to justify or fight it. It's a good sign if somebody dislikes or challenges what you do; it means your material is remarkable.

Remember this chapter the night you are crying into your pillow, wanting to give up.

INSTANT CHALLENGE!

Use the margins again to write down what you are sorry about right now; something you already know you might be guilty of doing.

Having done this, your fault is less likely to trouble you. It's even more effective if you publish a picture of it.

———

#salesengineers #accusationaudit #freemind

15

IMPRESSING PEOPLE WE DON'T LIKE

ELIAS SCANNED the laptop's clock the moment Maria joined their meeting. Seven minutes late. He told himself to relax; who knows what caused her delay?

"Hi Maria, how are you?"

"All good," she replied. Her video feed stayed black, just displaying her name. "How can I help you, my dear friend?"

Maria controlled what content got published on Sellingpower's blog and the ConnectedOut platform. Elias noticed a slightly negative tone in her 'my dear friend' phrase.

"I still can't see you, Maria."

"My bandwidth at home isn't good."

That was a pretext Elias hadn't heard for a while.

"Okay, no worries. I am planning to post articles about Sellingpower via my ConnectedOut account and wanted to ask if you could send me the handbook on our company's do's and don'ts."

"Great to see your ambition."

"Sure. All for the company, right?" As far as Elias knew Maria, he guessed she would disagree. Maria protected her marketing kingdom like a lioness protected her newborn.

"I can offer you three posts to publish right now. Oh, and

there's a recent one by our CEO about how numbers make numbers that you should like and share."

"Actually, I'm planning to create content myself."

"Yes, and you definitely should." Maria paused and coughed. "You have a lot to say, I'm sure. But believe me—and I have been doing marketing for over twenty years—just start with our approved content. Then you can grow from there."

She keeps me at arm's length and will never give me her blessing.

"Okay, Maria. I get your point, but it's not what I discussed with Ralf."

"And what you gossiped about with Ralf is irrelevant to me. There should be a very valid reason for us to start allowing inexperienced individuals to post about our organization. We have a brand to protect, my dear."

Here we go! I haven't started posting, and I'm already being judged.

Elias couldn't help but feel like a child. Deciding to progress on the thought leader path didn't seem to be enough. He needed to overcome so many obstacles that the universe put in his way. The relationship between him and Maria from the day they met some years ago. He didn't see any value in the current conversation, and not being able to watch her face gave the whole thing a weird touch.

Maria subtly disapproved of his idea.

"Then just send me what you have, and I will start with that."

"Good, give me a few weeks, please. Thanks, Elias. Lovely that a great person like you is supporting us."

Did she just say weeks? Elias ended the meeting and shook his head. *Really? What was that?* He wouldn't accept being blocked by Maria, and he swore that her boring, centuries-old content would never be shared on his feed.

I mean, I would post it. But I'm sure that she's just playing me.

Elias realized he would need to find a way to follow up with his promise towards Ralf by going around Maria. She didn't share the company's social media guide because there was none. That would open up Maria's realm for too many unpredictable challenges—maybe something interesting, controversial, or even provocative. That's not what Maria wanted.

———

AN HOUR LATER, Elias was still thinking about how to circumvent Maria's brick wall when Jessica sent him a message:

"Listen to Epictetus: Be content, then, to be a philosopher in all that you do (and to be seen as one), show yourself that you are, and you will succeed."

That sounded cryptic to him at first. After reading it the third time, he pictured Brad Pitt in a film whose title he forgot. Wasn't it even forbidden to speak about that movie? Either way, he remembered a quote that had sounded cool at the time but now appeared philosophical: "We buy things we don't need to impress people we don't like."

That's it! My first post won't be about the company; it'll be about me and how poorly I've handled obstacles in my way. And this post will mark my tipping point. I will start seeing obstacles as opportunities that push me to even higher levels.

16

THOUGHT LEADERS SEE
OPPORTUNITIES IN OBSTACLES

WHAT WOULD YOU DO IN ELIAS' situation when a roadblock like Maria tries to convince you of a different route? Would you consider this a situation that helps you progress?

Once you start on the thought leader path, you might dream of recognition from your peers and people who follow you because they admire the insights you provide. After all, that's the goal of that endeavor, isn't it?

But you'll need a rocketship to reach your vision.

It might appear to you that the astronauts who've already reached the moon—the successful thought leaders—write the perfect viral posts and get the speaker slots for the popular events.

But what got them to this point is often not apparent to an observer. Usually, we only see the outcome of the hard work and obstacles overcome.

There are examples of authors the media celebrated as overnight successes, but they wrote dozens of books before the first one took off. *Carrie* was Stephen King's eighth novel, not his first, and he crafted his writing rocketship his entire life to finally reach the stars.

Are you ready to work on your shuttle, even if it means

giving up a glass of wine with your spouse in front of your favorite streaming platform after work?

Another example is *Harry Potter* author JK Rowling. Her website[1] states she wrote her first novel at eleven. Now, look at the news about her. You'd believe that she decided late in life to start writing *Harry Potter* and instantly hit mercury.

How misleading is that when you look at your success? Think about what you have achieved in your profession so far, how crucial time was, and how many problems you had to overcome to build your skills.

Let's assume you had no idea about social media thought leadership or the influencer business, but a generous patron gifted you an email list with ten thousand followers. With that amount of influence, you definitely could build a living.

But what would happen when you started writing to them? Presumably, you would see unsubscriptions, low open rates, and little response to your calls to action. You'd likely fail to contact your followers in a way that resonates. An audience that you haven't built up and know inside out is tough to satisfy. Just as writers need to find their voice, you need to come to terms with your thought-leading vision. As Rowling or King were forced to master their craft, make their mistakes, and suffer rejection, you also need those obstacles to grow. Only by overcoming them can you win.

In Rowling's case, she attracted luck by not giving up and constantly submitting her work to publishers. It never works without luck, but don't be fooled into thinking that's all it takes. Attracting fortune means a lot of work: building the network, being visible, writing stunning content like articles, blogs, and posts, and on top of that, not giving up when people advise you to.

A sufficient supply of material for your thought leader shuttle might be tough to get. Although not many people aspire to become known—less than 1% of the 750 million LinkedIn users post weekly[2]—in absolute numbers, even this minority is overwhelming. So, there will be pushbacks and competition in certain areas. Podcasts will find your website too shitty to feature you, more prominent blogs will reject your guest author requests, and your newest post, the one that you're immensely excited about, will get only a handful of likes and barely a view or share.

It's like trying to make a brick wall fall over just by pushing against it. You need to chisel your way through. The cement needs to be removed before you can even consider pulling out a brick. The chisel will likely break; your hammer will be stolen, and on the other side, an envious person will be trying to put more bricks in the way.

Whatever happens, make sure you start again. Even if it feels like you've made no progress at all, you have. You restart from a higher level of experience, and that is all that matters.

Just continue and see obstacles as invitations to improve. They're an echo from the universe (or whatever term you like) that you're on the right path. On the other hand, you might be heading down the wrong path if things are too easy, no hindrances block your progress, and not even haters bother to share their ugly thoughts with you.

You are shaping your life. You are bringing energy into the world. Your roadblock shows you where to improve.

Just follow those echos and accept them as necessary. Overnight success is a scam. Don't believe it.

INSTANT CHALLENGE!

Use obstacles as a basis to create extraordinary events, which in turn will produce extraordinary results. Scribble some potential obstacles in the margins of this page and publish a photo of it.

#salesengineers #obstacles #extraordinary

17

A SAFETY NET FOR LIFE

THAT EVENING, Elias sat on his sofa with a glass of Amarone. Usually, he didn't drink, but after reading an article about great Italian wine that afternoon, he decided to try it. After all, he could use a bit of relaxation.

Enjoying the notes of dark chocolate and raisins, Elias looked out of his window. The tarmac was reflecting the street lights. A woman with an open umbrella went by, although it wasn't raining. Was Elias also employing an invisible safety net, just in case it rained in life? If so, he only used the equivalent of one hand to craft his future; the other clung tightly to his umbrella.

Looking into the sky, Elias realized clouds had pushed themselves in front of the half-moon. Suddenly, his thoughts went to Jessica. He squinted over his shoulder at his laptop, and before he knew what he was doing, he'd gone over to it and opened the lid.

Quickly, the bright ConnectedOut design appeared on the screen—the news feed, Elias' profile picture, and followers. He clicked the messages tab to answer Jessica because he'd forgotten to do so after Ralf's meeting.

'Thanks, Jessica. I am happy to accept your invite. Sadly, I have no idea what Amor Fati means.'

What am I writing here? I've had wine. This answer will sound silly when I read it tomorrow. Gosh, I shouldn't have done it.

Suddenly, blinking dots appeared. Jessica was online and answering. The blood rushed to Elias' head. *Calm down*, he told himself and refilled his glass with the delicious Amarone. He sipped and relaxed.

Then Jessica's reply appeared: 'Hi Elias, you're welcome. As a philosophy lover, you'll find out one day. Are you still in the sales team pitching to us for the CRM solution?'

Philosophy lover? What does she mean by that?

Elias scanned his profile and spotted the change he made some days ago. *Man, I have no idea about philosophy; I just love those clever quotes. In vino veritas*, he thought, giggling.

After another sip of wine, he answered: 'Still part of the team. We're preparing for the meeting next week with the steering committee. This time, I'll make a better impression.'

'Glad to hear it. Do you mind me sending you some advice regularly?'

What is she suggesting? Does she want to help me? That would be amazing. Why is she doing it?

'Sure thing. Are you offering to mentor me?'

'If you want to call it that, then yes.'

'Are you kidding? That's the best thing that's happened to me in months.'

Watch your Amarone tone! Should I apologize for being drunk? Well, no. Better not.

'Okay, your first task is to find out what Amor Fati means. See you next week.'

18

THOUGHT LEADERS HAVE A COACH

During Elias' hero's journey, a guide appears and tells him what to do. She is crucial to pulling the hero over the threshold and leaving the status quo behind. Elias isn't the happiest person on the planet. It's not that he is sad; he's just never thought about how he could change his situation.

Stoic philosophy says that you're now living the life of your choice. How you train yourself to handle circumstances is what you are. Do you get angry quickly? Do you blame others for situations in your life? Do you judge colleagues or prospects without really knowing them? Did you choose your job or your boss? More precisely and provocatively expressed: how you spend your day is how you spend your life. Sounds crazy, right? Sounds radical.

Maybe, but it's the frightening truth.

If you invest money in the stock market without following a strategy with discipline, you're just a gambler. The same is true in sports and military careers. If you want to swim at the Olympics, you need to train.

Your wish to become a thought leader or influencer won't happen without practicing writing, positioning, and focusing on your domain.

That's the first step: being willing to get your rear parts off the sofa.

The second step is finding out what exactly propels your skills. Real professionals leave most of the strategic planning to their coaches. They bring the outside perspective and a good amount of experience. Additionally, a mentor will provide you with a framework that leaves you no choice but to become successful. From then on, every day, you deal with the important things first.

Now you only need to execute, understand, and repeat—no wandering around, only progress.

Why then are people reluctant to invest money in mentors when it would help them progress in life? Have you hired a career coach to prepare for your job interview or propel your sales skills? How about a life coach? If you want to start discovering your strengths on a small budget, try the Gallup Strengthsfinder[1].

What would you think of a person telling you their goal was to win Wimbledon? You wouldn't doubt that they had a tennis coach to help them succeed with such an ambitious plan. But they tell you they're coaching themselves. Most likely, your estimation of this person's odds of winning Wimbledon would plummet.

So, do the homework needed to become a thought leader.

Envision the future of your domain and define a provocative problem statement. This will allow you to generate ideas. Then learn writing. Get beta readers for your texts, and pay professionals to review your style and language.

Get high-quality blogs, whitepapers, or even books out there. Have them reviewed and edited. Hire yourself a writing coach, a literary agent, or another author who supports you with self-publishing knowledge.

Then, learn to handle the soul-crushing feedback those well-meaning people will hopefully offer you.

Build a network and speak with other thought leaders and

influencers. Choose mentors from this group and strictly follow their advice. Show them the results you've achieved by executing what they've taught you.

Join challenges, grow by pushing your limits, and through the motivation the other participants give you.

You're not alone, and you shouldn't be. Every individual playing in the Champions League employs a coach, and if you think you don't need one, you're probably not a professional. So if you sit there thinking that an advisor is expensive and that this book is asking you to forgo your next vacation to pay for professional support, then yes, they are expensive, and that's what this book is asking you to do.

INSTANT CHALLENGE!

Scribble on the empty space of the page what kind of coach would make the most sense for you. Publish a photo of your results online—maybe you'll attract a mentor that way.

#salesengineers #coach #personaldevelopment

19

AMOR FATI, MY FRIEND

ELIAS LOOKED at the online documentation about Amor Fati, puzzled. The term seemed to originate from the German philosopher Friedrich Nietzsche. But modern stoics tried to attribute it to early stoic heroes like Marcus Aurelius or Seneca.

Somehow, Elias understood the literal translation of loving your fate, but he couldn't grasp the meaning. He thought of his parents. They had worked for Weisser Ring, a German association that supported crime victims and helped to fight online hate and harassment.

When Elias was four years old, his parents had received death threats. It became so dangerous that they had fled the country, and most likely been killed, leaving him with his grandparents in the UK. Elias never found out what happened to them.

I'm afraid of stupid social networks and could vomit when supposedly clever people offer their life advice online. How can I love the path my life took?

Philosophy seemed to be detached from life, so it wasn't surprising that nobody showed any interest in it. On the other hand, stoic wisdom resonated with Elias, especially the thought that the only things in his control were his reasoned choices: to seek virtue and to be good in life.

Elias didn't want to give up. He was looking for an idea to turn a post into a publication, so he read more about the stoics. It seemed most of their great minds suffered a lot: Marcus Aurelius lost children, and Nero even forced Seneca to commit suicide. Maybe those wise guys weren't that far away from real life.

Have we become weaker over the centuries? I'm sure we have. Modern people only need to get a headache, and they start whining.

Elias scrolled through ConnectedOut, where an article about Steve Jobs caught his attention. This typical quote-in-picture post was where the author added a 'True?' to the image and waited for likes to come in. But the intriguing bit was the quote used: "Love what you do!"

He needed to speak with Jessica about it. Time to build a relationship with her. Elias was interested in her opinion, so he called her.

"Hi, this is Jessica."

"Elias here." He stayed silent for a second. "I hope I'm not interrupting you. How are you?"

"No worries. I'm glad you called me, actually. What's on your mind?"

"Okay, listen. I'm looking for a topic for a post and want to investigate Amor Fati. It inspires me. I was asking myself if you do what you love?"

"You've read that quote from Steve Jobs, right?"

"Yes. Don't you think he is right?"

"I think he is. But most people misinterpret what he said. Look at it carefully."

"*Love* what you do," Elias read aloud.

"And what have you asked me?"

"If you ... *do* what you love."

"Exactly, Elias. People automatically switch the meaning to fit their comfortable life."

He wondered whether that was true for him too. Why had he become a sales engineer? It wasn't a thing he loved; actually, he hadn't heard of such a job before a headhunter had offered him the Sellingpower position.

I started loving it. Being in sales was tough at first, but then I enjoyed it more and more. Was it an unconscious thing I did? I wasn't planning to love it.

Jessica broke the silence. "And it's the same with posting online. Find reasons to love it."

"I'm a bit afraid of it."

"Welcome to the club. I'll tell you something; most people don't even know how intimidating it can be to put your opinion out there."

"But they have no issues with mean comments and disrespectful behavior." *Just like me.*

"As a creator, clinging to Amor Fati is the only healthy way forward. Love what you do and what life events it brings to you."

"Even if that means leaving your child?"

"What?"

"Sorry. That was uncalled for."

"No problem. It seems I triggered something," Jessica said with a soft voice.

You did. "Maybe I can find the courage to overcome my disturbing thoughts."

"Do it and wait for echos to come in. Use them as a new motivational push."

"The type of system that feeds itself. That's what I needed. Thanks, Jessica."

20

THOUGHT LEADERS ARE INDEPENDENT OF OTHER PEOPLE'S OPINIONS

Elias needed to learn that anybody who publishes anything is facing their fear. You never know what others might think, and most successful writers would advise you to follow this feeling of unease. James Altucher puts it like this[1]: "If you are not afraid of what you are about to produce in the world, then chances are it's been said or written before."

Nobody can be successful without support from other people. It's your network that opens up opportunities for business, fun, and growth. Someone points you in a direction that you haven't thought of before or introduces you to a person who removes a solid roadblock. Through a recommendation, you get into contact with an organization that you didn't even know existed, yet they crave your thought-leading ideas.

But there is a journey involved here, too, because your capability to grow through other people comes after you become independent. As a sales engineering thought leader, you've mastered your business's technical and sales sides, and as a person, you base decisions on your integrity and principles. The rule of thumb is that you add value to others if you are in a state of interdependence. This can only be achieved if you are independent[2].

For example, as a sales engineer, you should feel perfectly comfortable having a client meeting and playing the sales part, pitching their deck, having the business conversation, or fixing the next steps. That doesn't mean being the perfect account executive, but you should know enough to substitute them seamlessly in meetings when required. This will provide you with invaluable insights and make you professionally independent. This independence makes you a better team partner as no fear or doubt is limiting you, and you will be able to bring innovative approaches into the deal.

And, of course, your technical skills should be above average. Whenever you answer a client's question, the audience has to think your words come easily and that you have already experienced their situation.

The critical point, however, isn't to show off with your technical knowledge. You are a guide, not a poser. What you say should always mirror the business benefits to your client. Tech for tech's sake has no value for executives. So study techniques on asking questions[3], lead the client from the solution to the problem space, uncover the hidden issues, and provide real value.

A sales engineer thought leader isn't a breathing-and-speaking feature documentation!

Sometimes, you have to fight for this point of view. There'll be managers, account executives, colleagues, and even clients who won't understand why you don't just demo your software or run a feature presentation. But you have to know why. It's your reasoning that counts, and your long-term success is the proof.

Finding a mentor who supports and challenges you on the path to independence is massively helpful. Finding that person isn't easy, but as the saying goes: *When the student is ready, the teacher will appear.* So, don't wait for anyone and don't listen to other's opinions; craft your own and start working towards your goals.

INSTANT CHALLENGE!

Use the empty space to scribble down areas of your life where you could become more independent to enhance your sales engineering and thought leader career. Publish a photo of the page.

Independence is worth the struggle.

#salesengineers #independence #interdependence

21

TWO OLD GUYS IN HELL

TIFFIN TIME. Elias had invited Herbert into a web meeting to get his opinion on an idea, and he'd chosen the green-walled teahouse as his office for the day. Disappointment crept up within Elias because the usual waitress was a less polite waiter today. Her calm and friendly charisma were definitely reasons for choosing this side-office.

Breathing in deeply, Elias pressed the *share* button and gave Herbert access to a document that contained the draft of his post.

If I'm already nervous about sharing the draft with one person, what will happen when I publish it?

While waiting on Herbert to join the meeting, Elias glanced back and forth over his text. He was pretty proud of his brain-child. It was stolen from an older book by Maurice Joly, who had let Machiavelli and Montesquieu meet in the underworld where they philosophized about might and reason.

Suddenly, Herbert's voice startled him out of his thoughts. "Hi Elias, good to see you."

Oh, is there a slight annoyance in his voice? He didn't like my writing.

"Hi Herbert, how are you?"

"I've read your draft."

Typically German; straight to the point.

Elias nodded and said, "I know there are some syntax errors still. But other than that, what do you think?"

Herbert paused, sipping from his coffee pot. He never seemed to smile, and he didn't at that moment. Time stretched, threatening to tear apart. Elias heard people whispering in the teahouse, dishes clinking, and spoons being swirled in teapots. The strong smell of black tea found his nostrils.

"Well, it needs a bit more structure," Herbert answered.

Structure? What does that mean? Elias just stared at his screen but nodded politely.

"Your idea is not bad. So it seemed when you pitched it." Elias heard Herbert clicking with his mouse and stayed silent. "Machiavelli and Montesquieu meeting in hell and speaking about CRM. Some dialogues are amusing. So, there's something here."

"But something is still missing. Is that what you're saying?"

"Yes, and I can't put my finger on it. Have you thought of other characters? More modern ones?"

"What, like the Avengers?" Elias asked.

"That's funny. Iron man could be the sales engineer guy, and Thanos could play the VP of Sales."

"And they argue about CRM?"

"Now you got it, Elias."

Can this be true? His face slides into his palms and he massaged his temples. Elias was irritated. He'd already invested several hours, and now Herbert was suggesting a significant change. What was he fighting here? The effort or that his work wasn't good enough? The different spin on it?

"Listen, Herbert. I think I'll stick with my original idea," Elias said.

"Which one? The two old crocks talking in hell? Wasn't that this French guy's idea?"

It's amazing how quickly I forgot the source of inspiration and made it my own. I rediscovered it, nothing else. "Interesting. Yes, you are right."

"Everyone is stealing ideas; it's just important to give it your original spin."

"I don't think that's true. What about, for example, Da Vinci's Vitruvian Man? That is truly original." Elias was pretty proud of this finding.

"Stolen." Herbert said.

"Are you kidding me?"

"Nope."

"By whom?"

"Aunt Google is your friend."

Elias still wasn't convinced. "But Avengers would be your spin."

"And you merged it with Maurice Joly and created something completely new."

Why does it make me feel uncomfortable? I should delay that post. What a pity.

"Okay, I'll rework the text and give it more structure," Elias said.

"Great. Keep going; this looks really promising."

The call ended. Elias swallowed his pride and imagined how Iron man and Thanos would argue about CRM in hell. This version could work better. But it also felt to him as if a new door had just opened.

He looked up from his laptop as the door closed behind the waitress who just entered.

Elias smiled.

22

THOUGHT LEADERS ENJOY THE ART OF STEALING

HERBERT'S MESSAGE about the need to steal art surprised Elias. How do you feel about it, dear reader? Have you maybe experienced somebody using your idea? Let me give you some thoughts on how you could handle it mentally, in case it happens again.

Firstly, you might have asked yourself why the cover of this book features Leonardo sa Vinci's Vitruvian Man. Well, it's not only to give it a stunning look but also to bring home this very point: Leonardo stole the idea[1]. Around eighty BC, Marcus Vitruvius Pollio put forward the idea that well-designed temples are analogous to the proportions of man. Leonardo and his contemporaries such as Francesco di Giorgio and Giacomo Andrea then tackled this notion with drawings and thus produced the famous images of the Vitruvian Man.

Or take a look at philosophy and the great work of Marcus Aurelius, his *Meditations*. A big part of it is not original; it's a collection of other philosophers' ideas. And that is fine. He combined other philosophers' findings, connected them, and drew conclusions. It was his way of reminding himself of his very principles.

What about the Faust myth? A pact with the devil wasn't a

new idea. But Goethe built on the medieval tale, writing his wildly successful *Faust I* and *II*. Thomas Mann later wrote his famous *Doktor Faustus* based on the same myth. But all those works were original, weren't they? At least, nobody is accusing them of stealing.

Every artist was inspired by former masters in one way or another. Everything you read affects your writing and your opinion. The same goes for drawings. It *does* matter what you looked at recently when you start a painting. Do you surround yourself with nature? Do you mainly enjoy comics or the pictures of Monet?

Don't fool yourself; everybody is stealing. And you should steal, like an artist[2]. Combine your original spin with the work of other leaders or professionals. Build on them to reach new heights.

Another example happened in the 1920s. Theoretical physics was a hot topic, with groundbreaking progress in relativity and quantum theory. Einstein[3]'s ideas seemed truly unique, but he built on Newton's laws and Maxwell's equations. Einstein's work would have been impossible without them. He mastered former experts' theories to level up his game brilliantly.

Similarly, Niels Bohr[4] extended the atom model after Rutherford concluded from his gold foil experiment[5] that atoms have a nucleus. Bohr added that electrons circle in shells around the nucleus of an atom. His thoughts were novel and got rejected, although they were based on results from former thinkers. Even more, his model explained why atoms emit different colors based on their complexity. Einstein loved Bohr's thinking, although the foundation of it was stolen.

Be Leonardo da Vinci, be Niels Bohr, be Einstein; master a topic, steal, and adjust.

Everyone who is successful does it. It's just not always apparent because some artists steal ideas so old that they have been forgotten.

It seems even more evident if you take a closer look into the personal development and coaching realm. Every coach invented a twist on the same principle: take responsibility for your life and create something great.

On that note, please, take responsibility; read through this book and create something great as a thought leader!

INSTANT CHALLENGE!

From what you have read so far in this book, find something that is worth stealing and mark it with a highlighter.

Make a photo and publish it.

#salesengineers #creativity #serendipity

23

STOP CRYING

THE FROZEN PICTURE ON ELIAS' flat screen showed a beach polluted with tons of plastic bottles spiced up with dead seagulls and dolphins. *Plastic Planet*. He watched it regularly to remind himself that he harmed Planet Earth whenever he bought stuff wrapped in plastic.

He had to stop the documentary because Jessica called him. Laptop on his forearm, Elias walked up and down in his flat, complaining about his lack of success.

"Only one *like*, including my own," Elias said to Jessica.

His mentor smiled. "It was a good try."

"You knew that my idea of the interview in hell wasn't the greatest, right?"

"How could I know?"

"Then tell me what you know!"

"As much as people love original ideas, I think they want the simple stuff. The real stuff. Something sad or funny. A failure or success."

"But it's all in there!" Elias clicked his post and watched the statistics. 178 views and his own *like*. Should this be the result of eight hours of writing and editing?

"I know, and what you wrote is clever."

"Still, nobody cares."

"Regularity counts more than highly polished content. Give it time."

"I'm not patient enough for this."

"Why don't you start like a philosopher? You said you love it, right?" Jessica showed her bright teeth, and wrinkles appeared around her eyes. *She is damn charming.*

"And how do they start?"

"Like you, they ask questions and observe their world. But they don't act on anything untested."

"You are not making it easier for me, Jessica."

Why am I still trying this? It's too hard for me. Everybody tells me stuff; I'm not sure they even understand why it works for them.

"Your current post is too complicated, it doesn't trigger human emotions, and it doesn't use metaphors to be interesting to read and understand."

"Wow, that was frank."

"Now be a philosopher and test my assessment like a merchant in Greece would have done two thousand years ago. They would bite on that coin you presented to them."

"How many more hours should I put into this stupid endeavor?"

"Success is a stairway, Elias."

"What?"

"Stop this childish behavior. I thought you would be willing to shape your life."

Elias was shocked by her straight outburst. And he knew she was right; there wasn't any reason for him to complain. But still, it hurt.

Jessica broke the silence. "So, what's your philosopher's answer?"

Sighing, Elias thought about an answer while watching the ceiling. "Well, I do it because it's my own reasoned choice. What I've got under control are my skills and the effort I put into my goals." Elias noticed the off-putting image on his flat screen. "I have to be the change that I want to see in the world. There's no need to complain about people not liking what I produce. The only way forward is to create, hone my skills, and put myself out there time after time."

"Did you read that?" Jessica laughed. "Okay, so what's the truth?"

"I guess you mean that situations don't care about my feelings. Being sad about something won't change anything."

"Well spoken, Marcus *Elias* Aurelius. You may continue with your life." Waving, and with a big grin on her face, Jessica left the meeting.

Elias shook his head and suddenly started laughing at himself. He didn't care that he was so loud his neighbors could hear him.

24

THOUGHT LEADERS USE TIMELESS IDEAS AND STRESS METAPHORS

ELIAS HAS a creative mind that generates ideas a bit too far out to be digestible for other people. Of course, he should try everything out, but for consistency, thought leaders should connect their content with timeless topics.

Strong leaders resist the notion that their current generation is unique or better than the things that came before them. Although certain attitudes have come and gone, what people are always doing is living, dying, loving, giving birth, fighting, laughing, and crying.

Connect your audience with those timeless aspects of human beings. You bait sellers if you write about two sales-people arguing how to approach a client. Also, praising colleagues and showing genuine affection for others is worth sharing. If handled in a non-dramatic way, even a lousy day or a failure is a valuable read for most people.

We aren't special because we believe in knowing more and feel the urge to show off. On the contrary, the generations before us thought the same. And the generations after us will most likely do that, too.

It took Copernicus and several hundreds of years before humanity understood that it wasn't the center of the universe.

Has the human race accepted that yet? Take a look at the century-old proven theory of quantum mechanics. It seems odd how few people care about those strange things that happen day in, day out at the microlevel of our reality. Can you answer the question of whether light is a wave or a particle? Do you know how gravity influences time and space? Scientists answered those questions during the first half of the twentieth century. Indeed, today's most intelligent technology, like lasers, GPS, or magnetic resonance imaging, wouldn't work without it. We aren't the center of anything.

But this conflict of perception and reality might be a timeless idea for your content. Although proven wrong by philosophy and science, humans still believe they are the most remarkable thing in the universe.

TIGHTLY ALIGNED with timelessness are metaphors because some of them make it into our daily language. Just think of a mountain of work, the calm before the storm, or Mother Nature. A brilliant writer might have invented them once, but today, you as a writer should avoid them like the plague. Actually, that last analogy is a cliché, just like the metaphors before.

Metaphors are a sea of possibilities to express emotions and ideas to your prospects. Notice the cliché? Reread the sentence and think about an alternative way to express it.

But there are some disadvantages to them, so be conscious.

Firstly, metaphors don't come easy, typically because we aren't creating them often enough—we aren't trained. Except if you write professionally.

Second, most of them aren't timeless. To be "under pressure" stems from the time of steam engines. Giving "input and feedback" became part of our vocabulary in the computer age. And most of those sayings will disappear if they don't survive as a phrase in everyday language. To repeat that, in writing, you should avoid cliches.

Third, a metaphor might be way off from what you want to say.

Metaphors and comparisons are a science in themselves, and there are some things to be aware of.

If you want to stress that your product is high-quality, you could say that your product is reliable, like a garbage truck. Well, the garbage disposal guys and gals are reliable. They do one of the most important jobs there is for our well-being. But garbage in itself has a connotation that you should avoid when making a point about quality.

Also, it might not sound well-rounded if a metaphor takes too long to explain a process. Sometimes, a comparison can even be too close to what it is describing. Think of data cleansing software and a comparison stating that it automatically cleans your data like a vacuum cleaner robot scheduled to take care of your living room floor. That's a bite to chew on. It's too heavy and too close to the real problem—cleaning.

You should keep it simple, but if you compare an electronic locker with a safe, you are obviously naming a synonym, not using an analogy. Accepting those two pillars as boundaries will help you craft analogies that stick like an earwig.

To get a different spin on your metaphors, imagine software users and what benefit they would gain. A finance department might have great interest in some kind of unique data, and the mentioned software could be their "snowflake generator" as it only produces unique, duplicate-free data. You get the point: don't stay abstract. Go into detail, zoom in, and test different perspectives.

It'll take some work to effortlessly invent tested metaphors and comparisons that flow into your talks or writings. But they'll come once you focus on it.

Let's look at an example from the field: maybe you've had discussions with prospects who were merely looking to replace existing in-house software with yours. Those deals aren't considered to be strategic, justifying substantial time investments. Nevertheless, they are an opportunity to do fundamental discovery and qualification. To widen the topics discussed, you might want to (boldly or not) *reframe* the client —namely, convince them that change needs more than just replacing tools.

How would you pack that into a metaphor? Please feel free to contact me with your ideas.

An exemplary solution that worked in the field was the following comparison: "Don't switch the gym!" Some people have a gym subscription but don't reach their fitness goals. So they talk to themselves until they are convinced there's something wrong with their current gym. Of course, switching the contract won't make them slimmer. Still, it seems to be a common approach. The path to enduring results is changing habits, not switching the gym or replacing software.

The art in sales (engineering) is to detect the client's intent, desire, and urgency for change. Is your prospect merely looking for a new gym because they hope to get motivated by the new one?

Depending on your available resources, you should think about stepping away because you won't motivate them long enough to stay a happy, recurring customer. Is your prospect asking for a new way of working (which you hopefully offer), and is your software built to accompany that approach? If so, you are in the perfect spot for an engagement.

Speak with your audience by using metaphors and give yourself time to come up with them. Challenge yourself and your unconscious by collecting ten topic ideas daily and tag one of them to be a metaphor. Let them be childish at the beginning; they will mature over time.

Go to the (thought leader) gym daily.

As Arnold Schwarzenegger wrote in his biography, "Repetition, repetition, repetition."

INSTANT CHALLENGE!

Create two analogies and two metaphors that describe your business.

Example analogy: Replacing software in an organization is like switching gyms.

Example metaphor: A window into your technology.

Don't forget to publish your result so that we can like it.

#salesengineers #writing #creativity

25

HOW TO RESCUE PLANET EARTH

THE MOON GLANCED down on Elias as he closed his living room window. He didn't notice the pale ball as he was deep in thought after finishing the discovery call with a new prospect. As it was hard for him to decline a colleague's cry for help, he had taken over an opportunity on the other side of the world.

The potential customer had an in-house CRM application, but their field team wasn't using it properly. Elias wondered about that because the methodology implemented was stunningly cutting-edge. The prospect used AI to forecast the best timings for follow-ups, scanned professional networks, gave hints for personalized contact ideas, and provided relationship diagrams of people of the client's organization. The availability of such functionality in the market with the given maturity was new even to Elias.

Given that—and this was the point his prospect hoped Elias could help with—the field team entered crucial information so the AI could do its magic. But the sales employees failed to do it, either because they weren't motivated enough or didn't understand what they had to do.

They don't want to buy from us but rather learn our methodology. Is this what Herbert angrily calls free consultancy?

Of course, Elias didn't have a solution at hand, but he felt that there was an excellent opportunity to outsmart the competition. An intelligent way of providing deal-relevant information to the sales team paired with tooling employees want to use.

Elias took enough notes to think about a spin on the prospect's process. Then his stomach was growling.

"Time for dinner," he murmured while scanning his fridge. He found a plate of pre-cut vegetables, put it into the oven, and a few minutes later, the tasty smell of potatoes baking in olive oil flowed through his flat.

He lolled on his sofa, swiping through the feed on the smartphone. His current post had ten *likes*, and three of them came from second-grade contacts. "Invite them," Herbert told him all the time. "Don't wait for people to join your network. Be proactive and make them fans."

So Elias pressed the connect button. He had the option to send a message alongside his request.

How should I introduce myself? Something meaningless like "I would love to join your network?"

"Never start with yourself. Make it about the other person," Herbert's voice advised in Elias' head.

Should I say that I post on CRM topics? No, again, "I." Thanks for liking my post? Again, about me. Gosh, this is crazy. I will just send the request and think about it later. He invited the three people, and a woman from the U.S. accepted immediately. She wrote, "Thanks for your invite. I'm looking forward to our exchange on CRM topics."

Suddenly his oven's alarm went off, and he meandered through his flat into the kitchen. His meal was ready. Elias looked down at the chat on his mobile and up to his dinner cooking. *I need more time to answer.* He closed ConnectedOut and rescued his meal.

During dinner, he used to watch documentaries. He stuffed a huge piece of cauliflower in his mouth as he heard a person being interviewed in the movie say, "What's in it for me?" That struck him, and he realized that he wasn't watching but thinking.

Elias checked the title of the film: *Saving Planet Earth: New Insights*

What's in it for me? Is this guy really asking that? There's one little thing he should change to help save our planet. Why is that so difficult? And why can't we give a benefit to the people who act responsibly?

Elias unconsciously connected that topic to his discovery call some hours ago.

If an important topic like saving our environment couldn't help people overcome their ego, how could a CRM?

The prospect's process is definitely in salespeople's interest as it helps them earn more commission, but still, they aren't fully leveraging it. They reject change; it's simply too uncomfortable.

Elias was already typing his new post, titled *What's in It for Me When Filling My CRM—and Rescuing Nature?* Somewhere deep inside, he felt that there was a solution to this problem. He was sure it would occur to him if he worked himself deeper into the issue. It seemed that this particular question opened up the possibility for a range of new answers.

I should work on my skill to ask the right questions. That would not only make my discovery calls better but also my posts.

Like a philosopher would say, you grow the things in your life that you put energy into.

26

THOUGHT LEADERS ASK QUESTIONS

INTUITIVELY, Elias came up with a compelling insight. The quality of our questions acts as the mold for the answers we get.

Untroubled by challenging information, we humans stop learning and growing. Avoiding hurdles reduces our ability to ask questions, and we're missing out on the best feelings: the brain fireworks when learning a new skill or facing the cognitively uncomfortable.

Asking for information is troublesome, especially when you start as a sales engineer or thought leader. We want to give our best answers first, earning the right to be inquisitive. We might fear that asking questions makes us look silly.

It's no secret that our brain reacts to questions. Do you feel the urge to answer a question when it's directed at you? Yes? That's why authors and copywriters use questions to keep their readers engaged. That's why the best sales engineers run discovery meetings with their prospects and ask essential questions they prepared.

The sad thing is that our education discourages us from asking questions—especially questions that are uncomfortable or seemingly out of context. Teachers force children to learn the content needed to fulfill yearly plans. Questions outside the trodden path are usually not allowed because they endanger education deadlines.

Or, to quote Neil Postman, "We got to school as question marks and left it as periods." This observation nicely visualizes our (enforced) transformation from a curious person to a right-brain, analytical lexicon. Look around you in the professional world. Who dares to ask questions? Meaningful, constructive questions, that is.

There are those people who use questions to bully others. Stay away from such people and don't mimic them.

If you learn to ask questions, you'll automatically differentiate.

Especially in our role as sales engineers, we asking questions in a conversational, relaxed way is a crucial skill. But we unlearned it, and oftentimes, it isn't easy to use questions casually in a business context. It's not uncommon to judge yourself when you run a discovery meeting with a client. In those high-stakes situations with prospects, it actually matters if you ask silly questions—though that's not true for your prospect. Your reputation and perceived competence are in the line of fire. The best way to handle such a situation is to prepare meaningful inquiries.

As a thought leader and sales engineer, you can use questions in one more way: to reframe your audience. Visually spoken, a question is a template that the answer will fit into. If you want to convince your prospect of a specific thought pattern, ask a question that prepares your desired answer. Let's assume you're selling enterprise middleware software. Most of the time, your clients will want to speak about features, SDKs, IDEs, pipelines, code management, security, etc.

If your goal is to reframe the conversation and drive additional value by broadening the scope, you might want to ask a question like, "How easy is it with your current (old-school) tool to attract new talent?" Powerful question. If the answer takes longer than usual, you know you've hit a nerve.

You have a treasure trove of such questions at your disposal, but they sadly don't just spawn like your World of Warcraft character. You need to craft them by thinking daily and re-learning how to ask questions.

So keep in mind to use questions in the following ways:

1. To lead and engage your audience. We are triggered to answer when faced with a question.

2. To retrieve information. Learn to use them naturally and prepare intelligent questions.

3. To reframe your audience's opinion. Let the answer fall into the question's mold.

INSTANT CHALLENGE!

Use some space on the page to write down a question that you didn't dare to ask during your latest sales call. As usual, take a photo of the page and publish it.

#salesengineers #questionnotasked #salescall

27

THE DREAM

EVEN THOUGH HE had a busy week, Elias carved out some time every day that he would have used gaming to crystallize his CRM ideas into a text. Now he rewarded himself with a craft beer and the stream of a new documentary on his sofa. But it wasn't long before he was interrupted. In a good way.

Smiling, Elias switched off his TV and accepted Herbert's incoming call. He had sent him the final version of his new post ten minutes ago, and he was proud of the result. Its core message discussed why humans miss the bigger picture, lacking the motivation to act against climate change and, similarly, data entry in the CRM. Elias pointed out that the brain loves instant gratification, not some wishy-washy result in the distant future.

Still smiling, Elias held his beer into the camera. "Cheers. I hope you're impressed?"

Herbert looked tired and serious. "About what?"

"About my skills as a craft beer sommelier, what else?"

Herbert raised an eyebrow.

This guy always manages to embarrass me. It's the same style he uses in customer meetings. Is this his secret?

Elias sighed. "Okay, what do you think about the post? I

want to publish it before I go to bed."

"You should rework it first. Move your ending theme—where you mention the brain—to the beginning. Think of a bracket. And watch your tense. Also, some sentences are too complicated."

Elias gulped. Could this guy say something positive, too?

"And content-wise?"

"Yeah, it's okay. Rework it, and it'll be great."

Herbert is outrageous. How dare he say that!

With a pressed voice, Elias said, "I'll think about it. Have a good night."

"Of course, good night."

Some minutes later, still shaking his head, Elias walked up and down his flat. He thought about Marcus Aurelius and what a stoic would do. Control. The feedback he got was out of his control but what he did with the text was all his choice.

I will publish it. Screw you, Herbert. I'll prove you wrong.

Elias opened the laptop and hit the publish icon on ConnectedOut; his post went live, and he went to bed. It took a while until he fell asleep because his chest was tight. His parents' fate was haunting him, and he was afraid people would bully him, too. A soundtrack of thunderstorm noise finally helped him drift off.

Suddenly, he woke up crouching in a marble quarry. Touching the ground, his fingers felt the grainy sand. Close to him, a guy was swinging a pickaxe. He was as slim as his tool, and Elias couldn't see if his hair was naturally grey or just dusty.

"Where am I?" Elias asked.

"In heaven," the guy answered, shaking his head as if this was more than obvious.

"And who are you?"

"Stephen King, pal. Isn't that obvious?"

"Honestly, no. Good to meet you, and sorry, I've never read any of your books."

"Sometimes, it's good to stay on the side of the minority," Stephen smiled.

"Why are you hitting stones?"

"No, take a closer look. I am writing, my friend." At that moment, a huge marble block slipped out of the rock face.

"Ah, of course, you are." *Am I dreaming? I should stop drinking craft beer.*

Stephen threw away the pickaxe and took a chisel out of his pocket. Then he pointed with the tool to the marble block. "This is your current manuscript. What do you see?"

"A heavy stone?"

"Yes, what else?"

"A guy with a chisel?"

"Are you kidding me?"

"I wish I could."

Stephen gave up. "Pal, what you see here is the potential of a marble sculpture." He handed Elias his chisel. "Use this from now on, too."

"Do I look like a mason?" Elias asked.

"No, but you do look like a professional craftsman. Patience and quality should be your guiding principles." Suddenly the grey-haired guy turned into Herbert. "Iterate on your work, and it'll be great."

Elias woke up in the morning feeling guilty. His heart was beating, and he was confused.

What's up with me?

Immediately, he checked ConnectedOut. Ten likes, not bad. He reread his post.

Damn, syntax mistake ... I should rephrase that sentence ... My punchline doesn't come across that punchy.

Sighing, Elias took his post offline and corrected the apparent mistakes. Then he set a reminder two days from now to rework the text with fresh eyes.

Then his phone rang.

Smiling, Elias accepted Herbert's incoming call.

28

THOUGHT LEADERS BUILD THEIR WRITING CRAFT

WHAT TOUGH FEEDBACK for Elias to swallow. But at least he asked for it, and it's now in his control to act accordingly.

Professional writers spend most of their time editing manuscripts to remove distracting clutter. Every sentence acts as a necessary structural element. Each word brings a concept to life; none of them are wasted. An author of a book, a script, or a social media post strives to remove garbage until its valuable core is visible. In fact, authors say that editing is the process that makes a book great. The first draft of anything is shit[1].

Writers create art intending to be seen by a lot of people. They hope that millions will take time to read their work. Therefore, it should be a given to delay a release date for a month of editing, given that a book might be read for decades.

Follow this routine when you start writing regularly:

1. **Let a text ripen like a Ripasso.** Ignore the draft for a day, come back to it, and rework it, word by word, sentence by sentence. Strive for simplicity. Use short sentences. Be clear, focus on a single topic, and provide context. Give it time; there's no need to rush.

2. **Rework.** Ignore your reworked draft until you've forgotten what you wrote. Be reluctant. When you come back to it, remove the clutter. Look at your text with a critic's eye. Forget that you are the author. Forget the effort reworking puts on you. Then, strip your work down to the bones and build it up from there.

3. **(Optional but recommended) Pay for developmental editing.** If you are writing a book, hire a professional to get feedback on the structure of your work. Rework your manuscript according to the new insights.

4. **You might hate it, but you need to rework your text yet again.** This time, focus on style: be yourself, and express yourself. To achieve this, you must relax, and you must be confident. Put yourself in an expert's mood and enjoy the process.

5. **Now we enter the final round of editing.** This can be the toughest part. You open up your work for an external audience: for beta readers. The more confident you are, the more people you will want to ask for their opinion. They will come up with pages and pages of feedback. Judge for yourself whether you're going to implement all of it, but be sure that when beta readers find a bug, there is an issue. Look deeper. Rework.

6. **Editing and proofreading:** Finally, if you're planning a book, it's imperative that you hire a professional editor and proofreader. You can't do that on your own, and no professional author skips this step. The difference is simply how much editing is needed.

The magic behind this process is iteration. Think of tales: they got told over and over again, constantly being adjusted until they resonated strongly with us. It is repetition and refinement that make cultural trigger points tangible.

The iterative process is a successful and self-stabilizing concept in nature. Humans give birth to offspring with no input beyond another human—that's iteration. Our genes, for example, improve through iteration and disturbance. Mutation switches gene pairs. But over generations of gene iteration, functional patterns emerge that stabilize the complex system of our body.

You can calculate the factorial (!) using recursion, the mathematical form of iteration. All you need to define is the number n and a stop condition. Then you go: $0! = 1$ and, for all $n > 0$, $n! = n*(n - 1)!$. For 3!, the recursive solution would work like this: $3! = 3* (2 * (1 * (0!))) = 6$.

The magic of a self-inducing routine.

Writing good posts is a craft, not a divine gift. Those who write compelling stories repeated their process over a long time, outlined, failed, learned, and improved. They leveraged the power of iteration and trusted the process.

Read books on writing. Read books on storytelling.

Rework your stuff.

Learn to love soul-crushing feedback.

Your posts will become powerful.

INSTANT CHALLENGE!

Write down a statement that comes into your mind when thinking about technology, family, or career[1]. Got it?

Okay, now take the position of your enemy and write down what's wrong with this sentence.

Was that fun? Okay, now improve your sentence accordingly.

Done?

Write the sentence again as if you were shouting it from the rooftops. You should literally shout. Rework it until it works.

Finally, rewrite it in a way that only you could. Give it your personal voice.

When done, give your invested time some purpose and publish the result.

#salesengineers #yourway #creativewriting

29

SILENCE IS GOLDEN

A FEW DAYS LATER, Elias met Jessica when his account team presented a roll-out and implementation plan tailored to PeopleLove. The Sellingpower solution offered to Jessica generated sales reports based on the employee's performance. To be effective, each salesperson had to enter their respective deal information into the tool daily.

During the meeting, Jessica argued the problem with this suggestion was that the people entering the data couldn't see the bigger picture. The CRM's questions to the employees seemed either meaningless or missed context.

Jessica was furious about the lack of emotion in the solution. "Our problem is to be very specific; we don't want to stamp numbers generated by an AI on our employees' backs. But all your solution seems to focus on is supporting managers in justifying funding!"

In a new situation for Elias, Sarah's face turned pale. The way she raised her eyebrows meant she felt personally attacked. Louder than usual, she answered, "But the cost reduction in other organizations like yours is incredibly high with such an approach."

Jessica leaned back in her chair. And then what? Will we

find those numbers being used in performance reviews by our managers, intimidating our employees?"

Elias became confused when Sarah then started a fight. "Well, other customers of similar size to your organization find this a very effective process."

"I can't believe that. Why don't they just fire their best people immediately instead of torturing them with your process to the point that they resign?"

Elias had never seen Sarah speechless before, but there seemed to be a first time for everything. Maybe he should have been more confident too, as strategic accounts weren't just tough for him but for everybody involved. Including Sarah. Not that Elias thrived on other people's failures; it just gave him a little reality check. He sighed. This meeting hadn't gone as planned and could definitely doom the deal.

Suddenly, Elias remembered a feature he'd discovered two years back when creating this custom demo for a deal he eventually lost. But this one thing had stuck. Combined with the process he'd learned from his support-free-consulting call, Elias' mind formed a potential solution.

Stoic philosophy at play: We grow with our obstacles.

Elias smiled and said, "May I suggest an addition to the plan so that we also get the individuals on board?"

Like a cat, Sarah slowly closed and opened her eyes. Relief. As if an arrow had hit a balloon, the pressurized situation deflated with Elias' question.

"Sure," Jessica said.

Sarah nodded and seemed to silently pray that whatever came next wouldn't make the situation worse. But she kept her mouth closed.

"Our solution will gather a lot of information about your employees and how they run sales. And I get your point: to use that information simply to give them a performance number is intimidating. Would we add value if you could instead generate a strengths profile of your employees?"

With a curious look, Jessica seemed to wait for more. Elias paused and counted in his head.

One. He had learned from Herbert to create silence and to stay with it. *Two.* At least count to ten, was what he had taught him. *Three. Jessica was going to say something, wasn't she? Four. Just keep silent, mate. Five.* Sarah took a deep breath. *Please don't speak now. Six. Phew, she just sneezed. On mute. Seven.* Jessica leaned her head onto the right shoulder and added a suspicious look. He had to stay quiet! *Eight.* Jessica had to say something because Herbert promised that silence always worked. *Nine.*

"Difficult question, Elias. But yes, that sounds intriguing and would differentiate you from the current competition."

Sarah's facial expression merged a smile with disbelief.

Even Jessica enjoyed the situation, although Elias didn't know if it was because of the solution or just the way he presented it.

"Can we learn more about how you see that working?" Jessica asked.

"Can we come back to you in three days on that one?" Elias replied. She nodded.

30

THOUGHT LEADERS LOVE BLACK SWANS

ELIAS' idea was serendipity. He was lucky to have worked on the AI aspect of the solution and to have been presented with a client's problem that helped him connect the dots. By speaking to clients and hearing their challenges, he exposed himself to (positive) black swans.

But let's start at the beginning.

Being a thought leader also means doing things thought leaders do. Sounds obvious, right? But what are those things? If you want to become a professional swimmer, there's one thing you need to do daily: swim. Other people want to be runners, writers, yogis, or doctors. It's easy to see what their daily task should be.

You should think about what you do regularly and then throw out stuff a sales engineering thought leader wouldn't do.

First, they don't run canned software demos every day.

Second, they don't waste their precious time answering RfP questionnaires.

Third, they limit their time caring for tactical opportunities where feature and function discussions are the main reason to fight over the price.

What thought leaders do instead of those things is to craft their niche in the team. They focus on their strengths and develop a reputation. For example, if you sell finance security software and are skilled in fraud detection, developing a strategic workshop on that very topic might make sense. Next, you would offer that asset to strategic clients and train teammates on it. That way, your reputation grows, and you will be exposed to more and more strategic opportunities. That means you will meet more influential people with wide-ranging networks who will speak about you to others. You are creating a virtuous circle or a self-fulfilling prophecy that positively affects your professional life.

Basically, you do what Nassim Nicholas Taleb suggests in his book, *Black Swan*[1]. You expose yourself to positive black swans: unlikely situations that offer unlimited positive value. The idea is to increase the probability of occurrence by focusing on positive black swans and reducing negative ones.

There's a correlated question worth asking:

How likely is it that you will get a pay raise or become recognized as a thought leader when you only focus on standard sales engineering work?

Those chores might involve being the demo doll, answering RfPs, doing some coding, or answering urgent emails. Are you exposing yourself to positive black swans here? No, definitely not. Quite the opposite—chances are that management perceives you as replaceable, not only by other (possibly cheaper) hires but also by technology. The very thing you sell!

Just look at the map, *The Secret Kingdom of Sales Engineering*[2], to see what's happening in your space. If there are apps on it that you don't know, then things in your realm have changed and you need to get back up to speed.

But if you take a risk and step up, doing the things that nobody else does, then you will expose yourself to positive black swans. And this is what you should do. The more situations you craft that way, the more your chances of success increase. Positive effects of the risk-taking endeavours compound because your network and reputation typically grow with it. Soon, echos of your efforts will come back to you and carry you forward like the wind in the sails of a yacht.

Another way to find these positive black swans is by supporting peers. Don't ignore beginners; they'll grow. People have the potential to grow to the best version of themselves—this is what stoic philosophers believe. And who knows if your associate colleague will become CTO of a famous company in five years, citing you as their mentor? Positive black swan.

Another way to increase the likelihood of unlimited value is to carve your niche.

Who do you want to be? What do you stand for? Add value by investing in your skills and inventing new methodologies, tools, and content for your company. Apply it, and let it grow. Slowly but surely, reduce negative black swan work like demos and RfPs. Bring yourself in front of the C-level or run highly customized workshops for your strategic opportunities.

You will get known and remembered that way.

A helpful exercise here is to develop two mission statements:

1. Your internal one: How do you want to be seen by your colleagues? For example, "I am the go-to person about fraud detection, and I reframe strategic clients to love our vision and solution."
2. Your external one: "My customers perceive me as a solution-oriented and resourceful person who they invite to learn about cutting edge finance trends. Additionally, they think I love to pitch to C-level."

To a world of more (positive) black swans!

INSTANT CHALLENGE!

Scribble down the daily tasks that differentiate you from the crowd and expose you to positive black swans.

Publish the photo. You know the drill.

#salesengineers #routine #blackswan

31

WE AREN'T PSYCHOLOGISTS

"I DON'T BELIEVE the message will resonate with our customers," Maria said, wearing her typical smile. Elias stared in disbelief at the green wallpaper of the teahouse. Then he caught the view of the waitress, and she immediately gave him an honest smile. Surprised, he looked back to Maria's video feed. He suspected her behavior was a well-established facade. The marketing lead always seemed to be against proposals she hadn't brought up herself. Had it been Ralf's idea, she would have praised it and then found polite reasons either not to do it or delay it until everybody had forgotten.

Elias looked over to Ralf's video feed. The VP of Sales seemed bored. For him, all of this was child's play.

"I see, Maria," Elias said. "But I will need to get back to Jessica in two days. I asked you on the call not to say no but to look for a solution everybody could agree with."

"Elias, this is really honorable of you. But I don't think there is value in generating strengths profiles in our tool. We aren't psychologists."

"Assuming you're right, how do you explain the one client who does see the potential value? As you know, we are responding to a request from the field." Elias grew angry with Maria's way of protecting her domain.

She is toxic to the organization. Am I the only one who sees it? I wish she would at least talk to some clients.

Ralf chimed in, "Okay, cool down, everybody. There is a request from a client; you are right, Elias. But we should respect Maria's twenty five years' experience in the field."

It doesn't matter how many years someone has spent on a job. You can do crappy work for decades and get away with it."

Maria's fake smile widened. "Thanks a lot, Ralf. Why don't we reposition the deal with my...our 'Numbers Make Numbers' initiative? It's successful with lots of other clients. PeopleLove will surely benefit from it.«

Successful? Go and visit some customers. Your campaign is barely used at all.

"They won't. Let me post about strengths profiles." Elias was surprised by his words. They bubbled out without any thought.

Maria's smile disappeared immediately. "No!"

Ralf was visibly confused and stayed silent.

Elias' brain switched up a gear. "Maria, we should work together here. Clients are asking for something novel from us. They are fed up with the 'Numbers Make Numbers' slogan."

"As long as accounting benefits from it, we should continue riding this wave," Ralf said. "But I also agree that we need to listen to the market and try out new ideas."

"You won't allow this amateur to post about AI profiles in context with our organization?" Maria asked, red-faced.

Ralf took some time to think. "No, but I cannot forbid anything he does as an individual."

Thanks, Ralf! And what have I done to you, Maria? Is it me, or is your life really that frustrating?

Soon after the call, Elias ordered another cup of green tea, giving a big smile and tip. Watching the steam rise from the tea, he assembled the core structure of his post. Then he put it into a manuscript.

As he was thinking about the strengths profile, he realized that by using APIs to connect to customers' HR apps and personality tests, organizations would even grow the solution's reputation. Every API connection first adds value and then makes it tougher to remove the app. Also, companies offering personalized features like an ongoing, accurate profiles of their sales employees will attract talent. Elias guessed that it would nudge people into entering more precise information as it improved their artificial alter ego—their digital sales twin.

While Elias wasn't working on the post, he configured the Sellingpower instance to work in the way he envisioned. The nearly forgotten features could be activated and trained with a simple model.

After some tests, even Herbert was impressed. "I wouldn't have thought that you had such big balls, Elias."

This German directness…

32

THOUGHT LEADERS UNDERSTAND WHY PEOPLE FOLLOW LEADERS

RALF AND HERBERT are slowly opening up to Elias and his style. He might not understand the reasons why just yet, so let's take a look at them.

In work or private life, leaders inspire us to do things we wouldn't do otherwise. Have you heard the term *Columbus leader*[1]? In most organizations, recruiting follows methodologies and checklists that evolved years ago and were iteratively improved. Employees in hierarchical organizations love answers. On the other hand, asking divergent questions—those questions that challenge processes and beliefs—are seen as disturbing or outright blasphemy. As a result, if companies choose a risk-free approach, nobody challenges how recruiting is done and whether the approach is still the answer to the current question. This inevitably leads to hiring managers who know how to get things accomplished in known territory. With a map in hand, they can cross the Alps with their team because they measure divergence of the current state from the target and adjust the route accordingly to stay on track.

Christopher Columbus[2] didn't have a map when he set out to find a new route to India. But he had a vision. His only chance to get people to work for and with him was by inspiring them. A highly competitive market needs Columbus-style leaders. As a thought leader, you need to be inspirational, and rest assured that due to decades-old recruiting beliefs, there aren't many Columbuses in your organization. And if there are, you will know them by their reputation as an interferer.

Do you have kids? Have they ever asked you with an energetic, irresistible smile to jump on a trampoline with them? How often could you say no? At some point, you will find yourself jumping with your offspring, wondering how you came up here as you had something more pressing to do.

It might seem like a tiny example, but it is your energetic, irresistible smile on social media that will inspire your followers to perform things they wouldn't have done otherwise (albeit mainly in their heads). You carve out time and room in their lives for your ideas, nudges, questions, and provocative points of view.

And over time, that influences how your audience perceives you. At first, you are like a child; you have a small following, little interaction, and maybe no organic growth at all. You are contacting other people, asking them to follow you, share, and comment on your posts.

If you believe in yourself and stay persistent with your daily practice, this will flip, and people will become attracted to you once you reach a critical mass of followers, presence, influence, and familiarity.

So, post often. Don't worry about reposting your timeless ideas. It's fine; your new followers will enjoy the content. After all, it made your existing ones follow you in the first place.

Reach out to people who resonate with your message. Proactively connect with them. Jump on calls with them. Be interested in what they do. This, in turn, will attract more of them, and you will get an understanding of your followers.

People love leaders, and people love to be inspired. It's just the way of least effort; it's convenient.

You won't be able to motivate every follower endlessly. But

your true fans will stay with you for a long time. They aren't the mass, but using the Pareto principle, they're about 20%.

Become a leader by consistently developing ideas. Don't jump into answer mode like our recruiting department. Leaders are incredibly talented in asking the right questions, the ones that propel thinking, reframe the problem, and redirect to novel solutions.

Remember the key point that it's alright to steal thoughts from other leaders, merge them with your own, and give them an original twist. Einstein's relativity findings were based on Maxwell[3]'s equations, whose ingenious work, in turn, was based on Faraday[4]'s thoughts (which were disregarded and laughed at).

Lead with your point of view, be creative and bold, and soon you will receive echos. Use them as motivators to help you thrive on your journey as a sales engineering thought leader.

INSTANT CHALLENGE!

What vision makes you a Columbus leader? Scribble it down here, take a picture, and publish it.

#salesengineers #vision #leadership

33

JUDGMENT

'PUBLISHING IN PROGRESS. Thanks for using ConnectedOut,' the pop-up window on his display showed.

Elias sighed with relief. The configuration of the Selling-power instance for PeopleLove worked so smoothly that he'd finally decided to publish his ideas around the strengths profile. He wanted to ride his current flow-state.

Acting in the social world reminded him of when he aspired to become a successful trader. Every time he sold a stock, the stupid thing immediately went south and triggered the limits for an automatic sell order, which booked a loss. As if he was observing a stock's chart for an ongoing trade, Elias nervously watched his feed, constantly hitting the refresh button to update the view counter. But it stayed with fourteen views. He scraped his hands over his beard.

Fourteen? That's it? Once again, he refreshed the page. Fifteen. *What am I afraid of? Nobody is ever going to see my post.*

As Maria predicted, the post about AI-driven profiles wouldn't resonate with an audience.

Was I judging her wrongly?

Suddenly, he felt guilty for his mean thoughts about the

chief of marketing. But should his intuition have been this wrong? Was one failed post proving him wrong?

I could at least hit the like button for my own stuff. So he did. It felt weird to him at first. But suddenly, the views jumped to twenty six, so his post had seemingly moved into other people's feeds.

He'd cross-checked his writing several times before publishing. Still, he was afraid to glean over it again now that it was live. With a pulse like a jungle drum, he reads the first sentence. Although he knew it inside out, it felt as if he was seeing it for the first time.

Aloud, he repeated what the screen showed him: "Typically, CRM focused on managers as buyers who want to reduce risk or get performance data of their team to justify funding."

Wow, that sounds lousy. Why had Elias thought it was so clever when he wrote it? Flat. That's the word he would have used if this was another person's post.

That sounds more like a German regulatory file than a story!

"Instead, the CRM industry should shift their spotlight onto those who actually carry information into it. Give data purpose and show field team members their strengths and how to thrive by building on them." Elias closed one eye as if he were aiming at a target. Did this hit the mark? He wasn't sure.

But he promised himself that he would rework his next post more often. How could he reduce his fear of embarrassing himself by putting stuff out there?

I need to face my fears and ask Herbert for feedback again.

He hit the refresh button one more time.

Suddenly, a *like* came in: Jessica.

Elias smiled and thanked her silently with a nod. Minutes later, more people were attracted thanks to Jessica's help. What had she explained to him some time ago about his crazy idea of the interview in hell? Success is a stairway.

Got it. I am moving forward on this step, preparing for the next level.

34

THOUGHT LEADERS UNDERSTAND THAT SUCCESS IS A STAIRWAY

Elias has finally understood what Jessica had told him about the nature of success, and most importantly, it keeps him motivated. Of course, the stairway is a metaphor, but most importantly, it models (perceived) reality. When you start using it to explain situations you face—the long journey to success—it provides you with life-changing insights.

How is a typical stairway built? When you approach it, there's a first step you have to climb. This first hurdle is similar to the initial resistance when you enter a new field or start a new subject. Things just seem complicated and overwhelming. Nothing really flows by itself. It's a known fact from systems theory that when a system changes state, there is a stage of instability, and with it comes reduced efficiency. See it as a kind of entry barrier or a toll you need to pay to achieve change.

Once you've climbed the first level, you are motivated. But the nature of a stairway is that a step is flat for a distance. And the stairway of success can have endlessly spanning, plane-like treads. You need to work your craft routinely to reach the next step, and pushing forward can feel dissatisfying.

But then. BOOM! The desired effect manifests itself. To those around you, it will look like an overnight success. Well, you understand already that overnight success doesn't exist, and now you know that it just seems like it does due to the stairway nature of success. You needed to put all that effort in to reach the next level, only to face the next wide plane in front of you. And you have no idea how far you need to walk this time. But it doesn't matter because you've decided on one simple direction: forward.

The Stoics would say that there's only one thing under your control in life: your reasoned choice. When you approach thought leadership or social media presence, you might stay in the ranks of two hundred followers for a year without progress. Your posts might get no more than eighty views even though you improve your game. So you decide to invest money and learn from a coach; you watch tutorials, pay for courses, and hone your writing game. Still, weeks and weeks go by without significant impact.

And then, one day, you publish this post. You don't think it's any different than the other stuff, but it blows the roof off. You get 1,500 views on the first day, stepping up to six thousand over the next seven. Not bad for two hundred people following. Additionally, fifty new people join your network. You've reached a new level.

Now, you might think that you've cracked the nut. The coming weeks teach you the opposite because views stall at five hundred, and your follower count is glued at seven hundred. Still, this kind of success was a mere dream for you just weeks ago.

What's your next move, though? Right! You stoically move onward. Post by post, follower by follower, you approach the next level until you reach your top.

It will blow your mind.

INSTANT CHALLENGE!

Draw a stairway on a free area in this book. Then think about how many professional steps you have already taken and label them accordingly. Can you also name some steps ahead of you?

You know what's coming... Take a picture of the result and publish it.

#salesengineers #successisamarathon

35

A PIECE OF JUNK

THE GROCERY STORE would close in eight minutes, and Elias was the last customer strolling between the shelves. He put some bread into his shopping cart as his smartphone vibrated—at least ten likes, some comments, two new followers, and a message in his inbox. It seemed like the social platform queued all the responses to his post and sent them at once.

He scanned the comments with an interested smile. Tina: 'Nice idea, never thought about CRM this way.' Greg: 'Great to see you posting, Elias.' Thomas: 'What bullshit. Why does every bastard think he should publish his unimportant thoughts online just because it's technically possible? Leave this junk of content where it belongs: in your brain. That way, nobody needs to bother with this crap.'

Elias grabbed for the shelf behind him because he suddenly felt dizzy.

What's this? Why do people…who don't know me…talk to me like that?

With sweat on his forehead, Elias stared at his smartphone and reread the post, his fingers still clinging to the racks.

"Is everything alright?" the guy behind the counter asked.

"What?" Elias looked up at him, faked a smile, and nodded. "All good, thanks."

Breathe. I can't control other people's behavior. It's not about me, but about them.

The inbox also showed unread direct messages. Elias hesitated to look at them. What if this guy also sent him a hate message directly? But immediately, he decided to look the dragon into the eye and check his inbox.

No message from Thomas. Relief.

Instead, a guy named Tim left him a notification:

'Hi, this is Tim from HumanizeData. Would you be interested in a call? I like your ideas and would love to pick your brain.'

Elias wiped away the sweat that ran down his temples, curving along his jaw. Straightening his spine, he corrected his posture. The crisp bag complained with a crackle when he released his hand from the shelf.

HumanizeData? That rang a bell. He remembered that name from an account planning meeting he had accidentally joined last Wednesday. This other deal hadn't seemed to roll smoothly.

Is it a good idea to speak with Tim if there's a Sellingpower account team working with him already?

But on the other hand, Tim wanted to pick his brains—an informal conversation. Was he violating compliance rules here?

The guy behind the counter shouted, "Hey man, I need to close now."

Elias raised his hand to indicate that he understood. Then he placed his thumb and index finger on his chin and walked towards the cashier.

Should I speak to the Sellingpower sales team? What if I get the same result as with my request to Maria? What if they want to join the call?

Elias wished he could avoid the account team because he

wasn't interested in the deal, only the connection to Tim. He decided that if people made an effort to follow him, he should strive for a genuine relationship. It wouldn't bring him or Sellingpower any more prospects directly, but it would generate more champions.

Or was he lying to himself? Could he show off by making a difference just because he published a post? That would be a blow against Maria's arguments.

Stop! Don't be a Thomas yourself. There is no sense in working against Maria.

Elias pushed away all thoughts. He took a deep breath and some discounted sandwiches from beneath the counter.

'Thanks for getting in touch, Tim. What about having a chat tomorrow?'

"Couldn't you pay first and then message your girlfriend?"

Elias stopped typing, looked up, and smiled. "Of course."

36

THOUGHT LEADERS WRITE FOR THE LOVE OF IT

THE UNKIND MESSAGE from Thomas hit Elias deep and triggered hidden fears. You might also face similar feelings when the world reacts to your content. This chapter is aimed at helping you to handle those situations.

As a thought leader, you do more than posting content on social media. You present a new version of the future, provocative thoughts about the status quo, or unusual lessons from the past. Maybe you point out undeniable facts people have overlooked or even actively avoided.

Your content is successful when readers react with strong emotions. They might feel offended, pleased, sad, joyful, or inspired by the ideas you set free. This emotional reaction is reinforced by the love and conviction you express for your domain.

But what does it mean for you to stick your neck out from the crowd in this way? It means you will generally attract three kinds of reactions from people.

First, some will react in a positive and supportive way. They might even fall in love with your ideas and become die-hard fans.

Second, some won't care at all, not even raising an eyebrow.

And third, some will be haters, leaving unpleasant remarks and pulling your thoughts into the dirt.

The first two groups are easy to cope with. For the latter, it might help to repeat a mantra: "Haters show me that I'm hitting a nerve. Haters make me famous. I am on the right track."

You have to learn to accept negative feedback on your writing. But this is different from someone making factually false and defamatory statements, which isn't acceptable.

From a stoic perspective, there are several ways of handling this, depending on how you feel. If your soul feels crushed, stoics advise observing yourself and where your opinion comes from. Is it based on self-worth? Is your ego limiting you? Remind yourself that you aren't that important; an easy way to achieve this is to look at the stars at night. The breathtaking view proves how tiny we are, and any problems we have shrink accordingly.

The other way to look at it is to understand that those comments are out of your control. You cannot change other people. What they say is really about them and not about you. Stoics argue that even your body isn't within your possession. All you truly own is your reasoned choice. To find happiness in the situation and become content with it, decide on how to react. This is an opportunity to remind yourself of the quiet stoic virtues: wisdom, self-control, courage, and justice.

So, ask yourself what would be a wise, unemotional, brave, and just response to a hater. Don't replicate hate; be kind and solution-oriented. Ask for facts to unproven claims. Answer in a manner you would like to be spoken to in the first place.

You could also think about joining a society that fights online hate. Those organizations also offer training, and there might be cases you have to bring to justice.

As long as you enjoy writing content and it's not some work

forced upon you or commissioned, your readers will feel your joy and honesty. Professional copywriters are professional because they manage to sound honest even when they're only writing things they get paid to write. As you aren't a professional (yet), try to ensure two things: fall in love with your content, and write for the some-who-will-love-it audience[1].

INSTANT CHALLENGE!

Pump up your karma! Leave at least three nice, supportive comments on other creators' posts today.

#salesengineers #karma #comment

37

GAMING BUDDIES

Elias blinked. The low sun was gleaming over the edge of the laptop and directly into his face. In the video feed of the meeting, he saw himself: he looked like he was wearing war paint, a light streak shining across his skin.

The prospect, John, didn't seem to be on Elias' wavelength today. He wondered why because when they'd first met four months ago, they seemed to be aligned—John also gamed in the same online community like him, so they had immediately bonded. The moment Elias told him that his guild had replaced his warrior priest with a shaman player, John nodded, repeating, "I see, I see."

Elias was still digesting Thomas's ugly comment on his post too. His parents' fate was playing on his mind.

What was it that made people publicly react in such a mean way? Was it their frustration or unhappiness? Did they not understand the potential consequences of such behavior?

Although he still felt uneasy, the realization grew that the comment was only a mirror of Thomas' inner world. It was his own anger that Thomas was putting out there, and it had nothing to do with Elias.

"You still with me, Elias?" John asked. "It seems you drifted away there."

"Sorry, John. Yes, fully with you."

After an awkward moment of silence, John asked, "Can you share your screen and show me how it calculates the win likelihood? The sales operations team was very interested in that and whether they could manipulate the math behind it."

"Sure, John. Let's do that. But before I tackle it, have you ever thought about what happens when you use our solution to generate strengths profiles for your sales individuals? I believe this is a far more long-term strategy that will differentiate you from the competition and will attract talent."

Was it the sun-created war paint on his skin that just let him be that provocative? He knew that John just wanted a CRM to make his VP of sales and sales ops happy.

"Okay, Elias. I see the point, but I don't want to make this selection process longer than it needs to be. Can you show me what I asked you for? Please?"

Elias nodded. Something woke up inside him. Suddenly he knew that this prospect was not worth his time.

"You did *what*?" Even over the video feed, Ralf's head was glowing like a Christmas ornament.

"I spoke to Tim, the CEO of HumanizeData." Elias crossed his arms and leaned back in his chair. "He liked my approach and wants to continue speaking to us."

This new information turned the frowning face into a smile —one with dollar signs in the eyes. "Amazing, I will tell the team to take up their work again."

"Tim wants me to act as the visionary leader of our account team."

"Since when can customers demand which team member is working for them?" Ralf asked, switching back to furious mode. "Can't you brief the current team and let them take it from here?"

"Ralf, the whole concept is still in development, and Tim is happy to implement it with my guidance. If this works, we are going to forge a new niche for Sellingpower."

Elias didn't feel good speaking to Ralf like that. He had assumed his VP would be a master of business strategy. Or was the team management process and the sales pressure limiting his capabilities like blinders? Scratching his nose, Elias waited for a reply.

"What would Maria say?" Ralf asked.

"I don't know," he answered. Of course, he had an opinion —it just wasn't the most positive.

Ralf focused on Elias with a serious look. "No, it doesn't work that way. Help the team to set up an appointment with Tim. Brief them and then close *your* opportunities."

What?

38

THOUGHT LEADERS CHANGE THE CULTURE

ELIAS IS CHANGING how he thinks about clients, and his conversations with management are full of friction. His opinions are pulling him in another direction. This will affect the organization and eventually influence its culture.

Thought leaders act according to their convictions and call for a change in culture that is desirable for their followers. All their contributions to the community challenge the status quo, as breaking norms and rules is the only way to switch from one stable state to another[1]. It's interesting to write and speak about the past and what has worked before, but true leadership lies in painting a bright future. Of course, the number of people you can inspire to follow through with actions and implement the suggested future-shaping changes defines your success.

Here again, we see the definition of a Columbus leader. Let's discover an unknown world together. Does it exist? Who knows? But the potential rewards immeasurably exceed FUD— fears, uncertainties, and doubts.

Culture can be like rust on your car; if it's not taken care of, it will destroy the structure or lower your trust in it. You might avoid putting your feet on a specific area because you know there's only a thin sheet of metal. Maybe you become careful about allowing passengers to ride with you because you sense danger.

Culture can be like this, implicitly forming unnecessarily limiting behavior. It's as if your organization is taking a gentle posture to relieve (cultural) pain.

As a thought leader, you should point out those limits and suggest repairing the car or getting a new one. After all, the culture of a corporation seriously influences its results and its capabilities to innovate.

Of course, it would be truly provocative to question the need for a car at all. Maybe what's needed instead is some electronic engine-supported hand wagon. No matter your culture-correcting message, as long as it adds more value and some people fight for your idea, you are on the right track.

If nobody disagreed, your thoughts wouldn't be novel, and nothing would change. Keep creatively disturbing the cultural status quo. Your community needs you to do it.

INSTANT CHALLENGE!

What thoughts have you expressed recently that led to resistance? Why?

Document below, take a picture, and publish it.

#salesengineers #resistance #yourway

39

CLOUDY SKY

ELIAS WOKE up when his phone vibrated close to his cheek. He had fallen asleep on the sofa last night while working on a new text. Shaking his head, he looked at the empty beer bottles, and the laptop flipped open like a mouth yelling at him. His head felt like a beehive that defended itself against a bear stealing honey. Elias massaged his temples as he checked the time: 9:14 am.

His smartphone showed a message from John, a top-performing rep and AE on the HumanizeData deal: 'Elias, we'll get an order from Tim! Thanks for your support, mate.'

Elias frowned. *This is ridiculous.*

There'd be no further benefit for him than shaking some warm hands. Okay, it was a great success for Sellingpower, but it had depended on him. Admittedly, there was no point in chewing on it, but still, it felt unfair. Maybe this stoic philosophy thing wasn't right for him. They would argue that one has to detach themselves from the outcome—no matter if good or bad—as it isn't under one's control; only the process is.

During the following weeks, the process got harder for Elias. His ideas didn't seem to flow as effortlessly as when he'd started six months ago. Being productive and following your routine, even if you don't want to, needs discipline. He seemed to lack that ability and tried to motivate himself by having a beer while writing. The downside was that he was waking up later every morning, wasn't feeling fresh, and needed a lot of coffee before he got productive.

I'll empty the remaining two bottles tonight and then stop this. I should start a morning routine instead of adding hours to the evening.

Elias put his finger on the laptop's scanner and last night's draft appeared. With rolling eyes, he read it. It wasn't a bad story, but it wasn't good either. Ideas that seemed provocative months ago felt boring now. But was it just him, or did his readers feel the same way?

He looked at his follower count. He cared about this number now—a bit. Seven hundred additional people had requested to be added to his list. Not bad during such a short amount of time. Although, with roughly one thousand followers overall, he was far from being a so-called influencer. And the number of contact requests had gone down lately. Yesterday, he hadn't gained any new followers at all.

Suddenly, he remembered a hint from Jessica: if you can't make one follower happy, how do you expect to make one thousand happy?

Somehow, he felt like a sandwich thrown on the sidewalk, with pedestrians stepping on him. He didn't have control over the situation anymore. How to keep building success from here? His head was empty.

But it's crazy; my fear of putting me out there melted away. Would my parents be proud of me? But what good am I doing with this business-related stuff? I should save the planet. Maybe I can donate more money if I generate income from posting. But how?

Beep-beep. ConnectedOut was asking for attention. A new message had arrived in Elias' inbox.

Jessica had sent it.

'Hi Elias, I haven't seen much new content from you recently. You have to plan breaks or meditate to clear your sky from all the clouds. Once you've achieved that, do the ten-idea exercise. Looking forward to reading your next post. Good luck.'

What's going on here? I can't bear this any longer. I need a break. Or do I need a more sustainable routine?

Elias slammed his laptop shut and threw it into the corner of his couch. Everyone seemed to know what he was supposed to do or was offering their advice.

Other people were benefiting from his success with Tim. Why should he continue publishing his ideas when he didn't get rewarded? People were already losing interest in him anyway. He'd run out of steam, and his content didn't feel fresh to him anymore.

Beep-beep. Elias stared at the closed laptop. It couldn't have made the sound. He then realized that his hand was clenching around his smartphone. Had he unmuted it that way?

With a strained breath, he opened the ConnectedOut app and read. 'Hi Elias, how are you doing? We are running a podcast for CRM freelancers and wanted to know if you would become a guest on our next show. Cheers, JK.'

Smiling, Elias looked away from the mobile and out of the window. The sun was shining with only a few clouds passing by. Clear your mind first.

He stood up and grabbed his running gear. His head hurt, but he ignored it. As he laced his trainers, he couldn't stop thinking.

A minute ago, I wanted to give up. What I say has an impact. Echos are coming back from the stuff I shout out. It seems I have to keep going.

Ten minutes later, he was out in the park and enjoying a mild winter day. A thin layer of snow cracked below his running shoes. Steam puffed out of his nose as if he was a little chimney. He pushed his thoughts away, trying to think about nothing. Every doubt that appeared he imagined to be a cloud that he blew away. He ran faster, leaned forward, and cleared his sky.

40

THOUGHT LEADERS STROLL

ELIAS IS A RUNNER, finding peace of mind when his breath goes fast and his pulse is up. He can't think of anything else in this moment but his presence.

A calm and settled mind is a crucial ingredient for creativity. Think of muddy water clearing up or the winds opening a white curtain to reveal a blue sky. In those symbols lies power. Negativity, pessimism, doubts, or fears have no room. Or, to look at it another way, they are too tiny to be relevant.

Sometimes, you will get stuck. New ideas will stay away from you. Your posts may not get your intended message across, or your mind might feel more like a rock when the words don't flow easily. But how can you see clearly when your sky is cloudy and your waters muddy?

Great minds of the past said that an idea is worth nothing if it didn't come by taking a walk[1]. Get used to strolling around. Leave your smartphone, audiobooks, and music at home. Just be there for you, alone with your mind and maybe your dog. Concentrate on nature. Bees humming, cars droning, birds tweeting. Observe without judging them.

Try to feel what's doing you good. Is it the sunshine in your face, the wind pushing against your back, the snow cracking under your feet? Greet them with a smile. Remember things you are grateful for. Enjoy the smells around you. Blow away those thoughts of doubt that appear for all of us. Remind yourself of the stoic concept that there is nothing in your control other than your reasoned choice alone—not your success on social media, not even your body.

When you do that, you are meditating. And if you find it valuable, you might want to spend some minutes a day practicing sitting down in silence. Get an app and start.

Most people plan their days with to-dos. Be sure to be the one who also blocks time for walks and relaxation. Stick to this commitment to yourself and protect them. And then, during the break, nothing matters except you. Trying not to think about new ideas will see you bombarded with them. Be prepared. Take a notepad with you, write it down, and let it go.

A calm and settled mind is a crucial ingredient for creativity.

INSTANT CHALLENGE!

Time for a walk, isn't it?
   Take a picture of you strolling and publish it online.

#salesengineers #meditation #creativity

41

UNDER ATTACK

"This is crap!" the comment below Elias' article read. Thomas had written it. Again. Elias stared at his laptop screen. What should he do now? Like it? Answer it? The comment was not a constructive critique; it was trolling.

What would my parents do? And do I want to relive their destiny by fighting such dumb people?

"Oh my gosh," Elias murmured as he discovered that other people had liked that comment. Unknown and known. Even some colleagues.

Elias had only just got over Thomas' first comment, and now this!

Why do you do that? Let me see who you are.

Clicking on Thomas's name, he looked at his ConnectedOut profile. The guy was VP of Marketing in an ERP company, had over 1500 followers, and didn't post regularly. Elias couldn't see that he behaved like this towards anyone else.

That's weird. He seems to leave kind and friendly remarks all over the place, but not with me.

Then Elias spotted that they had one connected person in common. Could this be a hint? Sadly, he couldn't see who because he wasn't paying for ConnectedOut's premium version.

Elias hovered the mouse pointer over the follow button. *Is my unconscious speaking here? Well then, let's do it.* With a click, he followed his hater and would now be kept up to date on Thomas' activities.

Shaking his head, he closed his laptop and smacked his face in his palms. Thoughts of people laughing at him ran through his mind. There was also a subtle fear of Thomas and whether he might prove a physical threat. Tears began to form.

At that moment, he remembered a book Jessica had recommended him some weeks ago. It was on how to become a successful author. One passage explained that you hadn't created something relevant if you hadn't created any haters or enemies.

Didn't that mean he should be happy about the hurting comment? He didn't feel like he should. *Unfair*—the word hammered through his mind.

There is no fairness in art and thought leadership. The game must be unfair for me to succeed.

Nobody benefits from a fair game as everybody has a different starting point in life: skills, mind, body, and experience. Exact fairness would mean being unfair.

Suddenly, as if ignited, Elias rose and pushed his chest forward.

"I won't give up!" he shouted. "Your unfair and impolite comments are an echo that tells me I'm onto something. Get out of my way, or I'll drive over you!"

He smiled as he imagined Thomas as a cartoon character, flat like a leaf floating out from under a giant iron.

42

THOUGHT LEADERS CARE ABOUT THEIR COLLEAGUES' SUCCESS

THOMAS GIVES ELIAS A TOUGH TIME—AND you'll also encounter someone you don't know who doesn't like you for unknown reasons. Is there a way to mentally conquer that bad feeling? There is, and it's called karma. Maybe you know that sharing is caring. The more good things you share, the more followers you will attract. It's as simple as that, although it's not easy. That goes for the knowledge base in your organization and any social platform.

Generally, you should share to do good, not for admiration or praise. Love the process and do the best you can possibly do, but don't be emotional about the result. It's just a bonus that you're a role model of virtue.

So, share your exceptional demos, your pitch deck, your anecdotes, your special workshop insights, the inspiring book you read about communication, leadership, selling, or mindset —write a summary and send it to your colleagues.

However, it's not that easy to get people's attention. Unless you're a "bad" magician sharing the magic world's secrets, people won't be jumping up to hear what you have to say. As a thought leader sharing information, you have to convince people to spend time with it. A simple step is to not just copy a link to the bookstore in a chat but explain why it's worth the read. In short: make information relevant, and put the effort in so your audience can digest it easily.

Don't be afraid of crafting and sharing opinions. Most people don't want to act, and the majority never will. There aren't many creators out there because people typically care about themselves the most. They only worry about what other people think of them. You belong to a minority who actively shapes their future and opinions.

There are different types of sharing. One thought leader might swim through the waters of technology like a mermaid. Others might be entertainers, sharing anecdotes of business and life, or trying to convince their audience of a problem they don't fully realize. Those types correlate with the persona *you* intend to create.

Thought leadership means a different reality for you and another person. Building a business requires different content to creating a personal brand. Technology gurus aren't pitching the same way as business methodology speakers.

Content delivery will be different: how-tos, stories, anecdotes, surveys, whitebooks, videos, books, manifestos, or even a lottery.

All those measures are different but have one vital aspect in common: high quality. Please don't confuse this with perfection, which can never be achieved. Instead, define a quality standard that is right for you and design a process that helps you get there. This will also alleviate the unavoidable doubts that will arise. Don't hit that *publish* button immediately.

Find out what you stand for, and take care of your community or customers with your fantastic content.

If you have trouble finding your persona, treat yourself to a challenge. Join our newsletter at https://saleshero.training to try our next one. A contest is an excellent way to get inspired— as it involves a network of people on the same journey and the beginning of a daily routine towards success.

INSTANT CHALLENGE!

Log in to your social network and say thanks to a colleague.

———————

#salesengineers #social #thankyou

43

SPARROWS DON'T COMPARE

PART OF ELIAS' routine was to spend his first productive hour of the day in his beloved tea house. The nice waitress didn't work that early, but he was fine with that because it meant less distraction. After optimizing a description in his profile, Elias scanned his feed. A very nicely written post about coachability caught his attention.

Wow, this guy has 13,000 followers, Elias thought as he inspected the author's profile—a CRM admin called Mark Watson. Crafting such a following must have meant years of work. With quick fingers, Elias scrolled through Mark's newsfeed.

Eyes still on the screen, he reached for his cup of tea but missed and spilled some. *Ouch!* The hot liquid burned his skin. Angrily, he put the tea back on the table.

He focused on the admin's content again. A post appeared that began, 'During the last six months, I developed a daily habit of posting, and here are my results. –Read more–'

Elias was proud of his achievements so far. He had attracted at least seven hundred new followers and felt that was an honorable result. But there it was—a silent feeling of uneasiness.

With a click, the post expanded.

Elias' eyes skimmed over the lines. In disbelief, he frowned.

Impossible!

This guy claimed to have gathered 13,000 followers in six months! Elias slumped back into his green satin armchair, which squeaked in concert with his battered ego. He caught the waiter's eye, who immediately smiled. *Even this guy is laughing at me.*

Suddenly, clouds of doubt appeared in his mind. What was he doing wrong? How could Mark, a guy with such seemingly trivial messages, gain so many followers in such a short amount of time?

Elias leaned back, his head on the back of the armchair, staring at the ceiling. An ancient chandelier stared back at him.

This social media crap doesn't make sense! I've been slogging away at this for six months too. Where's my success? I don't even dare to dream of 13,000 followers.

Elias closed his eyes and observed his heartbeat. Flashes of light sparkled before the eyelids, and noise rushed in his ears. All of a sudden, he calmed down.

Comparing yourself to others doesn't make sense. I attract a very niche audience by intent.

And this Mark guy was indeed working hard. One post per day, every day. Elias didn't have that kind of routine. Not yet anyway. But he could change.

Yet, he also wanted to be known for high-quality and focused articles, not just spam and inspirational quotes.

I'm on track. This is not a sprint for me; it's a marathon.

Maybe Elias would still be around even when Mark ran out of steam. And even if he weren't, everything would still be good.

The Stoics would say that other people's actions are beyond your control, but you do have the power to react to the situation with your own reasoned choice.

Elias pushed himself out of the chair. He opened his writing app and started a new post: 'Why You Spill Hot Tea into Your CRM!'

On the other hand, that kind of competition is quite motivational.

Now, he smiled as his fast-typing fingers poured his thoughts into his drafting file.

"THERE MUST BE MORE I can do to improve." Elias watched two sparrows in front of him, picking through the snow to find food. He walked alone through the park, clearing his sky again.

"Here, guys." He broke some bread crumbs off his sandwich and threw it over to the little birds. They chirped and ate hectically to get as much as possible into their little beaks before the crows came to steal everything.

Was working faster like the seemingly hectic sparrows a solution? Publishing more articles in a shorter time would give his audience more food for thought. But how to maintain the quality? How was Mark doing that?

Elias pulled his smartphone out and read one of his own recent posts. The content and general idea were good, but they didn't flow well. The read was bumpy, and he stumbled over a sentence that had seemed clear during writing.

What the hell does that sentence mean?

His skills still weren't where he wanted them to be. Maybe Mark had learned his craft on another platform first?

Elias went even further back in time, reading his first article. Laughing out loud, he caught the attention of an old couple. The sparrows flew away.

He felt some relief. What a gradient! His first post now felt amateurish and embarrassing.

The vibration of his smartphone interrupted his appraisal of his older self.

The podcast recording that JK had invited him to join was starting in an hour—time to go home.

44

THOUGHT LEADERS SEE
COMPETITION AS A STEPPING STONE

ELIAS' ego took a hit when he saw how successful Mark the admin became in such a short space of time. It's demotivating, to say the least. But don't give up; push your thoughts of failure away, and as Elias did, let competition become your motivation.

Let's also look at it from another angle...

There lies a great opportunity in executing everyday things in a differentiating way. This marketing rule is valid in your role as a sales engineer and when leading with your social brand message. But being different is easier said than done because it means fighting traditional wisdom—*we-have-always-done-it-this-way* thinking. How tough is it in your organization to completely dismiss a demo script, the approved proof of concept approach, or the RfP process? Those standard processes hold opportunities for differentiation if you're brave enough to challenge them. Why not have the client implement the PoC with you as a coach? Why not ask the prospect to replace the RfP with a value-adding workshop? Why not use domain-driven design's[1] context map[2] as a discovery tool[3] instead of using the standard oral and inquisitorial approach?

The main reasons why you want to think about differentiation are because the client will remember you, and that puts space between you and the competition. It might feel like competition is everywhere and the world would be so much easier without it. Your product shines during your demo, but you're caught off-guard when a client objects because a competitor made them doubt the quality of your solution behind the scenes.

Because competition lies outside your control, you can use the mantra that competition is a gift, not a burden. It helps you find your company's weak spots, so you don't need to invest time in it—whether directly or indirectly, clients will show you. Usually, a fierce competitor means there's a market for your product *and* your original ideas.

Consider a day in your sales engineering life:

You are widely positioning your product in your industry and often face the same competitor when selling to your prospects. What (hopefully) happens early in the sales process is that you—the sales engineer—run a discovery session. Your sales engineer colleague in the competing organization will do the same.

Your goal could be to simply milk more information from the client to gain an advantage. To achieve it, you ask for longer meetings. You could try, and it might work. But that also means your focus is not on the client and their problems anymore; it's based on flawed competitive thinking—how *you* can gain more information than the other side—instead of understanding the client to be ultimately resourceful.

For example, you could differentiate in *how* you perform a discovery. It's not a single session anymore, but a highly professional process with a discovery result document and a readout to the stakeholder. Additionally, it involves interviews with all organizations and their leaders who would benefit from the changes you suggest.

And instead of saying, "We need a 45-minute discovery session," you would announce early on a 'client engagement process' that is proven and leads to the best outcomes. This approach shows your prospect that you will go on a journey with them; you position yourself as a guide to achieving the best business results. Your mantra is "Dear client, here is the engagement process of how we make you wildly successful."

In summary, you not only use the discovery results to build a good demo but also to position yourself as a professional person in how you run the discovery process. You lead by still keeping the primary focus on the prospect.

Now mirror that to outperform—or better, differentiate from—other thought leaders in the realm of social media. If you don't have the power to develop as many topics as your peers, try instead to change how you deliver your message. Write humorously, invite weird guests to your live streams, wear crazy hats, only allow VIPs to read your stuff, or always post at five minutes to midday.

Honor your competition as intelligent and well-meaning people, but don't study their content. Don't give them a stage in your head or clutter your feed by fighting with them. Ride *your* bicycle, look at the tire in front of you, not the one next to you; plenty of crashes happen that way. Deliver your unbiased content, and use a differentiating trail if the current one is too crowded.

Trust in yourself and your ideas. Or, as Rocky Balboa[4] once told himself in the mirror, "You see this guy staring back at you? That's your toughest opponent. I believe that's true in the ring, and I think that's true in life."

INSTANT CHALLENGE!

Grab your pencil and describe what competition means to you.
Does it make you feel uneasy, or is it motivational?
   Publish your idea as a simple text post.

#salesengineers #competition #discovery

45

HEY, MATE!

ELIAS CHECKED THE TABLE. Tea? Check. Water? Check. Nuts and cucumber? *Damn, I forgot the walnuts.* Today, he couldn't go to his favorite teahouse as it would have been far too busy an environment.

JK, a forty-year-old surfer boy, spoke to Elias but looked sideways, probably to some podcast equipment, "Three… two…and we are live."

Now JK was all in. His voice was full of positive energy. "Welcome to the *We love CRM* podcast. I'm JK, and I'm proud to introduce our guest today. It's Elias Grant, Sales Engineer with Sellingpower. Welcome, Elias. How are you today?"

"I'm a bit nervous, JK."

"No need to be, mate. I discovered you on ConnectedOut some weeks ago. You wrote about something exciting that we will cover later. Do you want to introduce yourself?"

"Sure. I am Elias Grant; thirty four years old. Single. I love brown ale, am a vegetarian, a huge role-play game fan, and I wish we would treat our planet better. My all-time favorite game is *The Witcher 3.*"

As if the fog lifted, Elias' awareness cleared. What was he

saying there? Who cares what he eats or plays? He straightened his back and took a deep breath.

"Well, I never got into games, though I've heard about that one." JK laughed. "But let's switch to the topic our listeners are really interested in. What's your CRM journey and point of view?"

Gosh, I should have prepared better. Where should I start? With Sellingpower? I shouldn't name Maria, but I could speak about issues with marketing, couldn't I?

With his heart beating in his throat, Elias could barely concentrate.

Clear your sky. He closed his eyes and relaxed. Looking up again, he began to explain:

"Two months ago, I was running mainly product presentations to potential clients. The kind of chore a sales engineer has to do, you know?"

In the live-streaming window, Elias saw JK smiling. "Been there, seen it all," he said. "But I guess you changed something, didn't you?"

"Luckily, my demonstration failed on one occasion because I couldn't answer a tricky question."

"That doesn't sound like a situation I want to be in. How did you solve it?"

"Well, I had a kind of eureka moment when I tried to bluff my way through. Serendipity. I explored a new perspective of how our clients should use CRMs."

"What was the client's question?"

"Basically, how could they prevent putting meaningless AI-generated numbers on the employee's back to justify funding."

"What's wrong with that?" JK laughed and leaned towards his microphone.

This indirect question was one that Elias had never answered out loud. His response was vague. "Well, it's not human." Elias paused. "You need the support of the people who fill the CRM and to ensure that those numbers don't dehumanize them."

"I see. And what's your solution?"

"A new way of leveraging AI that makes sense of the given data."

"That sounds very cryptic, mate."

Elias smiled. "The point is that the data must primarily support the employee who's using the tool, not the manager looking for budget arguments."

Silence. JK seemed to give Elias room to think and elaborate.

"And a perfect way to do that is to create strength profiles based on the sales data. When you look at the effectiveness of salespeople, you can tell whether they're good communicators, creative people, demonstration experts, or fast closers."

JK chimed in. "Interesting, I've never thought of it that way."

It appeared to Elias that most professionals stuck to the way things have always been handled and had issues switching gears—or thought patterns, for that matter. And he hadn't even spoken about the concrete solution; he'd just marketed the problem.

"Look, JK. CRM professionals don't even seem to be aware that they're being confronted with this issue. I mean, why are employees reluctant to enter data?"

Laughing, JK said, "There are thousands of reasons, mate."

"Because it doesn't benefit them is the most important of all. A personal reason to do it is needed. Currently, the data is only for the sales manager, and you know how rough the winds of sales blow."

"You can bet on that one. But at least there's the side effect of great waves."

Elias smiled as he imagined JK on a surfboard and Ralf yelling at him, "The data you enter can and will be used against you. Think of all those account planning meetings where you got screwed because your sales calls seemed to be delayed and make you look lazy."

"Yeah, I had this one meeting where an account executive got tortured by a person who reminded me more of an inquisitor than a VP of sales." JK played a fanfare sound. *Tatataaa.*

"You got it. What we can do, given the right technology and knowledge, is solve the issue by creating strength profiles. This will help the field staff to understand their core capabilities and to focus on them."

"Great stuff. Let me ask you …"

46

THOUGHT LEADERS CREATE THEIR OWN CATEGORY

HOW DO YOU CREATE A CATEGORY? In short, solve a problem that nobody knew existed or solve a problem that was thought to be unsolvable. This is exactly what Elias does when he points to the challenge of motivating salespeople to enter data into the CRM. He even agitates the description and sticks his finger deeper in the wound. He keeps going until he reaches a point where he's positioned his solution. By leading with a unique insight into a problem, Elias crafts his own category.

All the big players, like Uber, Salesforce, or Apple, did the same.

But not only them. For example, take a look at the new applications entering the sales engineering arena, reducing the daily chores that have burdened professionals for so long.

One of those new players on the Sales Engineering Map[1] most likely will become the category king and take over 90% of the market. The long tail will sit behind the number two and get the remaining crumbs. The point is that new categories are in the making. You can watch one of the players, Walnut.io, who are actively positioning their "sales experience platform[2]." Their CEO, Yoav Vilner[3], definitely understands category design.

In the same way, thought leaders create content and think of their domain. A German influencer, Dina Brandt[4], brings a provocative point of view to the forefront, bashing the old-school behavior of boomers. And it works; she attracts like-minded people. She also attracts those who challenge her ideas, making it even more interesting because they start arguing in her comments. Her style is new, fresh, and different for a social business network, much more personal than most people; she writes in German and focuses on culture with her message. It's very clever, and it fits her personality.

Meanwhile, in America, James Altucher evangelizes a side-hustle game to his followers, speaking about how he hit the bottom several times but then built up an empire by trading, self-publishing, podcasting, running a newsletter, and adopting a daily routine. His approaches are non-traditional, and he crafted his own "unconventional entrepreneurship" category. Of course, James Altucher has a lot of money at his disposal for all kinds of commercial pushes, but either way, he carved his niche. Without that, all the marketing budgets in the world couldn't guarantee an engaged audience.

There seems to be a feeling that luck is a big part of such undertakings. And indeed, it is *part* of it. But conventional wisdom would draw luck and skill on the same axis and throw out numbers like 40% luck and 60% skill, which leads to arguments like, "She had 90% of luck, so her success is based on 10% skill."

That's a flawed perspective because luck and skill are not on the same axis[5]. They're not the ends of the same stick. The truth seems to be that on the luck side, the odds for everyone around the table are the same. This poker analogy explains that the most skillful players improve their odds over time. Their success doesn't depend on the cards dealt.

Skill development lies in your hand. Always have an eye on the long-term results, ignoring the urge to achieve something amazing quickly—that instant gratification our brain craves.

We have to take care that our luck isn't dependent on external factors. Becoming the best version of ourselves is one way of achieving that.

To quote from *Play Bigger*, a book about category design, "If the odds are the same for every company, your company needs to make decisions and implement a strategy that gives the best chance to beat the odds and beat competitive companies." Imagine that the odds mean the amount of luck involved in an endeavor to start a company. Like at the poker table, we all play with the same cards and are dealt equally unfairly. (You can replace the noun 'company' with a thought leader.)

So, learning about category design is well worth the effort because it advises you on how to play with the cards you've got. You might not win every game, but you will learn to be successful in the long run when you put the effort in.

Be realistic about how much luck is needed to succeed in your endeavor. Then ignore it, and make intelligent, long-term decisions for your content and positioning.

It's on you to build a long-lasting foundation and a category you will dominate.

INSTANT CHALLENGE!

Come up with three ideas for a category you can be the founder of. Start by thinking of a problem that either didn't exist before or is thought to be unsolvable. Once you've listed your categories, take a picture and publish it online.

#salesengineers #categorydesign #creativity

47

THE GRUMPY NEIGHBOR

ELIAS SLOWED DOWN on the icy slope that led out of the park. Carefully, he slid up to the sidewalk. There weren't any cars on the street today—another typical car-banning Sunday. He smiled because he loved the feeling that people were starting to change their minds about the Earth's health. Every Sunday helps.

Some old, frozen leaves cracked under Elias' steps as he approached his apartment. His mind wandered. As usual, it started crunching ideas for posts he could publish. The idea generation process was a thing he felt comfortable with by now.

But how can I get my ideas in front of more people?

The first association was speaking at an industry event. About eight months ago, he'd presented on stage for Sellingpower. That was the last time he'd spoken in front of real people instead of a screen. Since then, Sellingpower had massively reduced their travel budgets as they pushed their 'Online is the New Offline' campaign.

This definitely wasn't Maria's invention; she loves traveling and being out with colleagues.

The account executive role was hit particularly hard by the

travel restrictions, and complaints were loud and harsh. Elias thought his sales colleagues would start a rebellion soon. But interestingly, the company had experienced very positive results.

Anyways. Maybe I can get a conference speaker slot. Even if it's virtual.

The thought of public speaking, even online, made Elias nervous. But it was a different kind of nervousness to the crowded hotel conference room.

I can't hide anything on a stage. The resolution of real life is so much clearer and more terrifying.

Since his appearance on the podcast two weeks ago, his success and hunger for more had grown. Elias pulled out his smartphone and checked the web for CRM conferences. A lot of them were online only. For companies arranging them, the concept was much cheaper, and they could be held more often. But only some high-caliber conferences had established their names in the CRM domain. One of them was called "Love for Salespeople." This event asked for speaking proposals via an online form.

Until that day, Elias hadn't realized that the company behind Love for Salespeople was PeopleLove. Jessica's organization.

Should I ask her if I can attend? Would she agree? But why not?

Elias had implemented every task and hint she'd given him to work on. His writing had become much better after using storytelling techniques. His style had improved by copying texts written by authors he admired—even before he wrote one line himself. He visualized his success; he learned about marketing, positioning, category design, stealing ideas, and using philosophy to stay mentally healthy.

In front of his house, he turned around and looked over the empty, icy town. He took a deep breath and thought, *Is that life? Just living your thing, trying to have a good time? I got happier by taking risks. I'm building something.*

He unlocked his front door. His grumpy neighbor pushed past him, squeezing himself outside before Elias could enter.

"Hello," Elias said.

The grumpy guy pulled his eyebrows down in his frowning face.

Elias shook his head. "I wish you a good day, too."

You don't want to end like that. Don't stop shaping your life.

As he walked up the stairs, he spoke to himself, "It seems I'm the best speaker PeopleLove can get on stage this year."

Ten minutes later, he wrote a note to Jessica, asking for an opportunity to attend the conference.

48

THOUGHT LEADERS LEAD AND INSPIRE OTHERS

ELIAS IS SLOWLY TRANSFORMING into a person who wants to influence other people's thoughts. That's why he's taking every opportunity to speak to an audience. But how does inspiration work?

Have you noticed the sheer number of websites focused on wise, philosophical, and inspirational quotes? Just google "inspirational quotes." There are so many images, blogs, and websites offering nothing but timeless wisdom. No wonder business influencers publish them regularly on their social networks. Typically, those quotes are cleverly arranged words from a (usually dead) famous person on being a great leader. Of course, they're motivational, but can they provide guidance? Is the context in which the person initially made the quote applicable to any other context?

This is not to say all such quotes are useless. But overuse in any new context diminishes their value.

If you aspire to thought leadership, you shouldn't rely on quotes. It might be tempting to repost some wise person's knowledge. But how do you differentiate and lead with original content?

Thought leaders stress and adapt their message until it

resonates with their audience. Your goal should be that others quote you! The rebel idea you start your journey with might initially only be a feeling, but you get people interested in listening to you. Suddenly, feedback flows in; you find logical mistakes and improve preciseness.

This is where you should be open and flexible.

"Technology alone won't make you successful, dear client" is a perfect example of a provocative point of view. Not every salesperson would dare to say that when selling technology— even though it's true. In this conflict lies the true power of leading with thoughts. Provoking and reframing the prospect needs boldness. You're not working against your company.

But what is it then that makes thought leaders successful? Try to answer this question: what differentiates you or your company when you don't allow product features to be used as answers? A good candidate explanation is your exceptional process of solving a traditional problem in your industry. Your novel methodology is what your client needs to change their organizational habits. Your industry insights are just as valuable as your product, if not more. You teach your client a new way of thinking, and your technology just so happens to align perfectly with it. You show your prospect the next possible level of their development.

By quoting Johann Wolfgang von Goethe, this book's own rule is broken to support the argument: "Treat people as if they were what they ought to be, and you help them become what they are capable of being."[1] Apply that to your prospects and followers, and you will surround yourself with the most remarkable people.

INSTANT CHALLENGE!

Write down three provocative points of view about your area of expertise. What are you selling? Now remove the technical value. How do you add value to your client's people and processes? Why is that unique, and how does it challenge common wisdom?

Once you have your three, publish a text post about the one that resonates most strongly with you.

#salesengineers #pointofview #valueselling

49

LET THE EXPERTS DO THEIR JOBS

'Number 10: CRM applications dehumanize the sales team and therefore limit the company's success.'

With a smile, Elias glimpsed at the sheet of paper where he had scribbled down ten ideas for his PeopleLove keynote speech. Reveling in the joy of what poured out of his mind, he sensed that his provocative point of view would draw the audience's full attention. If he had learned anything from dozens of social media posts, an average opinion didn't excite people, only a polarizing one. Some readers would call him stupid; others would love him.

The green walls of the teahouse definitely helped him think. His favorite waitress was working today, and she brought him his tea. "How are you?" she asked.

She never spoke to him directly, so Elias was caught on the wrong foot.

"Sorry?" he asked. "Oh, yeah. Good. Excuse me, but I have an important meeting," he said, pointing to his laptop.

"Of course," she replied, nodding. No smile.

Wow, I am grumpier than my neighbor. What's up with me?

He placed the device in front of him and checked his emails. He chose the one from Ralf titled 'Keynote prep' and hit the link in the invite, happy to have got his ideas laid out just in time. Entering the call, Elias saw Ralf and Maria in the video feed.

VPs among themselves. Am I their juggler?

"…focus on our current campaign," he heard Maria say after he connected his audio. "Hi Elias," she immediately added with a big white smile.

"Good. Everybody we need is here. Okay, Maria. Elias got us on stage at PeopleLove. How do we tackle that opportunity, and what are we going to speak about?"

We? How do we tackle that? Why does he ask Maria? He should have asked me! Baffled, Elias stared at the screen. He waited to see how things might develop.

"Well, I think we should strengthen our 'Numbers Make Numbers' campaign."

No way! Elias couldn't resist chiming in, "Maria, the reason I'm there to speak is that I'm challenging exactly those kinds of traditional messages."

Maria stayed surprisingly calm. She answered with a smile that didn't reach her eyes. "And I don't know if you are aware of the fact that your current social media efforts cost us hundreds of thousands of dollars in marketing because your propaganda works against our campaign," she said.

Propaganda? Really? Elias couldn't resist countering. "Agreed, it's better to burn a marketing budget like yours with some old farts."

Oh shit! Immediately, Elias got pale and started sweating. This insult wasn't intended. He'd gone too far this time. *She makes me so angry. I should say sorry.* But he couldn't, his mouth was dry, and his tongue felt heavy. He wanted to grab his cup but feared he would spill it again. Better to sit through it calmly.

Maria swallowed his comment. She had over twenty five years of experience in marketing, which was good. Her resistance to keep herself up to date with things like influencer marketing, category design, or growth hacking was the main problem. It seemed she was just spending an immense amount of dollars pushing a campaign that fell as flat as a cheating soccer player—one who got a red card rather than a penalty kick.

After several seconds of silence, Elias found his courage. "I'm sorry, Maria. It's just… no offense meant."

"None taken," she replied in an angry voice, proving her answer untrue. "So, we need to bring our campaign back on track, and we've decided to let you do that."

Elias nodded. "I've prepared some ideas. We should take the time to look at them, so…"

Ralf interrupted him. "Elias." He paused. "You're doing an excellent influencer job. But you're a sales engineer, not a marketing employee. You will form a team on stage with John."

John had broken every sales record last quarter and won the deal with Tim. He was a sales superhero, but he only drank down the lukewarm marketing soup Maria warmed up for him.

"Did Jessica agree to that?" Elias asked with surprise. *Jessica got me on the gig for my novel thoughts, not decades-old brain farts.*

With rolling eyes, Ralf replied, "Yes, she knows about you teaming up."

What? Have they spoken to her behind my back?

"Ralf, if we speak about our boring Numbers-Make-Numbers thing, it risks our relationship with Jessica and the PeopleLove deal!" Elias said.

Maria couldn't stay silent any longer. "Don't call our campaign boring! Months of work from a lot of bright people went into that."

That doesn't make it more interesting.

But he agreed that his attitude was arrogant. Just like the way he perceived John, the sales superstar.

"Sorry, Maria. Again. Can I at least put some of my ideas in there?"

Ralf shook his head and remained silent.

Looking as angry as a dragon from a fantasy game, Maria looked into her camera. "I don't mind what you think, Elias. And I don't need your excuses. Just do what you get paid for and let the marketing experts do their job."

Red-faced, Elias looked up from his laptop. The other guests and the waitress stared at him and then turned back to their own issues.

"Sorry for being rude," Elias said to the waitress with the teacup in his hand. Then, he took a sip and relaxed.

50

THOUGHT LEADERS UNDERSTAND
CREATIVE DISTURBANCE

IT SEEMS like Elias just can't get a break to do his thing. At no point do his plans execute flawlessly. Of course, this is why stories like his are interesting, but it's also true in life. What he doesn't know is that disturbance lets us find truly novel ideas. Limitations make us more creative[1].

In corporate organizations, there is always high internal pressure to maintain the status quo. As a result, employees avoid process pattern changes and the accompanying risks. Yet, a process pattern is foundational to an organization and its inner workings. So, changing them is terrifying because they question established behaviors. But moving to new patterns is crucial to reach a new level and stay relevant in the market.

Instead, the optimization of existing processes is a core desire of employees and most managers. However, there's a difference between optimizing current capabilities and making a process pattern change.

To compete in international markets, every member of an organization needs to develop the skill of making process pattern changes[2]. To enable a company's transformation, the status quo needs to be disturbed; the organization needs instability. The skill to consciously create this instability lies in allowing innovation and mitigating the risk of a crisis.

The willingness to break old behavior is mainly bound to employees' personalities and their own reasons. They have to understand it in their own context and less in the corporate one. That's why people in organizations seem to disagree about how certain goals should be achieved—like Maria and Elias having opposing views on how to approach their market.

Novel thinkers bring a vast benefit, although they are often labeled as interferers. Their creative disturbance brings about the instability that's needed. Those employees help the organization develop a new process pattern that will produce more innovative results and make them more competitive.

Instability needs to be managed. Therefore, organizations need visionary leaders to inspire their employees to find a new manageable path through unknown waters. That's why they're called Columbus leaders[3].

Sometimes, unwritten rules need to be broken by them, but they understand that this is part of a strategic injection of creative disturbance.

As a thought leader, you are most likely disputing the status quo. Maybe you're challenging how your organization markets products and services. As a pure software company, it might be tough to find non-technology-related messaging like "Technology alone doesn't make any of our clients successful." But what else does? You are a creative disturbance for your organization that will eventually lead to a better understanding and adaptation of your offering.

As a critical voice—an interferer—you knew you were a minority, but now you also realize your importance.

INSTANT CHALLENGE!

Come up with three stressful things you would like your organization to change. What would happen when those patterns were disturbed? What would that change enable you and your organization to do?

Set a calendar reminder to revisit this page in three days' time. Craft a text post and publish your thoughts.

———

#salesengineers #instability #change

51

THE WET SHIRT

"Numbers make numbers, ladies and gentlemen," John said as he elegantly crossed the stage. A grey suit over brown shoes. His white shirt's collar was open, hinting at a well-trained chest formed by weights.

Elias stood at the edge of the stage, watching and waiting. Soon it would be his turn. Bright spots blinded him, and he couldn't see the crowd in front of him clearly. He realized that the seated audience was scattered like mushrooms in a forest. In addition to the four hundred attendees in the hall, many more listened behind screens. Three movie cameras were pointing at the stage.

John suddenly stopped and drummed with both fists on his chest while saying, "And we from Sellingpower are the number experts. Look, you can't measure what you control as long as..."

A rush in Elias' head stopped him from hearing what was said next. But it didn't matter because he knew the boring message. It was all about being better. Fluff marketing stuff that strengthened the competition rather than setting Sellingpower apart as something special. Maria and her team weren't growing their niche, just competing in the existing market. That had nothing to do with leadership or innovation. Despite the boring message, John entertained the crowd amazingly well, and his talk went down smoothly, so most of the audience enjoyed it.

He is a damn good public speaker. Elias sighed. His stomach felt as if he had just eaten raw eggs. John would finish his part soon. Elias grabbed a bottle of water to wash away the bitter taste.

As he opened the bottle, it slipped out of his hand, hitting the floor and rolling towards John. Whispers and giggles filled the hall.

With an angry look towards Elias, John kicked the open bottle from the stage.

Elias felt heat rising to his head, sweat coming out of every pore. He tried to fight the reaction by talking to himself.

Calm down. Breathe. If he didn't relax, the sweat would be visible on his shirt. Under his arms, on his chest and back. But it didn't help. Soon, the shirt clung to his skin, and a huge spot enthroned his chest.

I shouldn't have agreed to this peep show. It's a mess.

From the corner of his eye, he saw Jessica taking the stairs on the right, making her way towards the backstage area. She didn't look amused. Understandably, because 'Numbers Make Numbers' wasn't what she had expected. It was the exact opposite. Elias knew it and felt like a coward. He should have pushed more for his approach: rewarding the individual entering data and not the manager who needed numbers to justify their performance. It seemed that Jessica hadn't realized John would be serving up the Sellingpower standard show; she didn't even know who John was! He wasn't on the PeopleLove account team.

Did Ralf lie when he said he'd spoken to Jessica about the conference?

Finally, Jessica appeared at the side of the stage, invisible to the audience. She waved her hand to get Elias' attention until he couldn't ignore her anymore. Elias looked at her and grimaced a sad smile. Apparently, Jessica was furious. Her finger went across her neck as if she was cutting it with a knife. Then her lips moved, glowing like lava. Elias couldn't hear but read the words from her mouth. "Do something about that. NOW!"

His mouth was dry and his head was empty.

52

THOUGHT LEADERS ARE MENTALLY PREPARED FOR BATTLES

Wow, Elias is in deep trouble, and nobody can help him except himself. What would you do in his situation? Have you gone through the mental training that would prepare you for such a battle?

No matter how great a strategist you are, and no matter how good your plans may be, reality will hit them hard. Those unwanted situations might even hurt you emotionally, as your plan, your baby is being attacked.

Ray Dalio, for example, made it a habit to learn from every mistake he made and each success by turning them into principles. When he encountered a similar situation, he took his own advice and acted accordingly. Ray documented the learnings of his life in his book *Principles*[1]. You, too, should have an aphorism, mantra, or saying that helps you (mentally) survive stressful situations.

We make poor decisions if we feel attacked. So we need to find a way to be prepared in case the storm is above us. The most important thing is to remember your aphorism and correct your thinking accordingly. Try to separate yourself from the situation with mantras that you find helpful.

There are some examples of different life events here. Feel

free to take and adjust those you find useful. Ignore those that don't resonate with you. It's important that you define your own set of mantras.

When the going gets tough, the tough get going.

In situations where you need to be brave and you think all is lost, this saying could infuse new energy to continue. Elias' stoic version is similar: *Don't be an idiot and do what's right — courage, wisdom, self-control, and justice.*

Extraordinary results come from extraordinary events.

Know the feeling when you want to be praised for a specific piece of work? Dream about giving a TED Talk or founding your own company? Remind yourself that those extraordinary results don't happen overnight and need extraordinary efforts —no matter what the get-rich-and-successful-quick scammers might tell you. What was the last extraordinary thing you did to achieve an extraordinary result?

To do is the same as to want, only crasser.

Post regularly. Sometimes, a focus on quality will hold you back from doing what needs to be done. Getting out there is important. Don't overthink it. Every time you procrastinate, remind yourself of this mantra and just start.

I will promote myself, no matter what.

We all aspire for success and want our ideas to be seen and acknowledged. On social media, in particular, this only works if you are in the spotlight because that way, others will speak about you and share your content. At the beginning of your journey, though, you are unknown. You're unlikely to get a wide reach or a lot of shares. So, you are responsible for promoting yourself. Doing so might feel odd, but just think about this: would you hit the l*ike* button on your own posts? If your answer is no, remind yourself of the mantra, then think about how else you can get yourself seen out there.

Memento Mori.[2]

Memento Mori is the stoic term for reminding you of mortality. Everything in your life is borrowed, and the borrower might want it back any minute. So don't live your life as if you're immortal. Be grateful for the people around you, for the successes you had, and for the failures that taught you life lessons. Do good things! No matter how much time you are given, you can always fill it with doing good, being just, and becoming wiser.

Amor Fati.[3]

This is another stoic term for accepting your fate. Whatever happens to you, it's life's way of teaching you something. Most of the time, you can't control what happens to you. But you can choose how to react. And the Stoics advise loving what happens to you all the time as that is living in accordance with nature. Accept the challenges life expects you to overcome and become the strongest version of yourself.

Forget your ego.

If it's about you, it's most likely not about the world around you. Ego is your enemy, as Ryan Holiday observed. Leave your ego at the door when you enter a meeting and sweep it from the table when you read a great article by a competitor.

Obstacles are the way.

Another Ryan Holiday gem[4]. A bodybuilder would look like other mortals if there weren't big obstacles on the barbell that he is willing to push daily. The same is true for your personality. Look for obstacles and work through them to become the best possible version of yourself. Remember, the things that happen to you are neutral, and only your judgment makes them good or bad. Put another way, the situation doesn't care if you cry; it simply wants you to grow, so accept the challenge.

Who knows everything forgives everything.

This is a great saying that you should remind yourself of when people are offensive and impolite. You never know what happened to them today or in their lives in general. Don't judge too early, and do assume the best in people. Let the best intention become a self-fulfilling prophecy so that people are compelled to show you their best side.

How I spent my day is how I spent my life.

This powerful aphorism should remind you every minute to create value for yourself and others. Do good, do just, and become wiser. Living those stoic traits means living a good day, hence a good life. No matter how long or short.

Everything passes.

Every emotion passes by with time. Nothing lasts forever. So, no matter how you feel right now, assure yourself that it will blow over.

Start with selling a dream; you will be asked for the technical details later.

As a sales engineer, prospects and team members expect that you can talk about products and solutions at the deepest level. And of course, you can. But that doesn't mean you should do so immediately. Your knowledge, experience, and creativity are far more valuable when you first paint a vision. Show the art of the possible. Sell the client a dream first, and once they are hooked, explain the details.

Be the change you want to see in the world.

Nobody smiles; nobody cares about you? Your account team doesn't do discovery or deep qualification? Prospects are just items in the pipeline, purely numbers? If you want any of that to change, be the change. Smile, take care, discover and qualify, and act with integrity.

Success means having a plan, working to a daily routine, and making mistakes.

This aphorism works like a blueprint. First, make a plan of what you want to achieve or what you want to be. Maybe a published author? Then, you need a routine. Ask yourself what writers do: most likely, they write. How often? Daily, most likely. So, from now on, your routine is writing daily. Then you need to grow. As you learned above, we grow through overcoming obstacles. So, be bold, allow mistakes, and learn from them. This blueprint is bulletproof.

Successful people are healthy!

Have you ever looked up to someone and admired their power and achievements only to find out later that the person struggled a lot because they overworked and became psychologically or physically ill, maybe even both? Remind yourself: that is not success because it isn't holistic. Success means your whole life, not just the business part of it. Disclaimer: This is not to say that those with disabilities and illnesses can't be successful. By no means.

Look out for echos.

There will be moments during your thought leadership journey when you will think you aren't successful at all. Take a step back here and look for echos that have already come back from the market. Were you invited to guest blog, did you speak on a podcast, did people just follow your account, or did you get likes on your posts? Echos everywhere. Look for more, document them, and let them be your motivation. Don't stop!

INSTANT CHALLENGE!

Write down three of your life mantras. What are the values and principles you live by when things get tough?

Take a picture of your result and publish it.

———————

#salesengineers #personaldevelopment #principles

53

COURAGE, WISDOM, SELF-CONTROL, AND JUSTICE

BRIGHT SPOTLIGHTS BLINDED ELIAS. He barely could move, but he observed how a heatwave within him ignited in his head then spread throughout his body. Gulping, he squinted at John.

His highly praised colleague gestured wildly and ended his part of the presentation. "Now it's time for my sales engineering colleague, Elias, to continue with the 'Numbers Make Numbers' campaign, telling you about a *fantastic* customer case."

The semi-true story. With a questionable outcome.

John walked over to Elias and made a disgusted face as he observed the big sweat spots on his shirt.

Elias forced a smile on his lips that didn't reach his eyes. He took one little step forward and stopped.

"Go, it's your turn!" John whispered through closed teeth.

Elias couldn't disregard the orders he got from Ralf and change the presentation spontaneously... Could he?

Another tiny step.

On the other hand, he didn't want Jessica to perceive him as a weak character—a Stoic always strives to become the best version of himself. It was PeopleLove's conference and, therefore, somehow Jessica's. He and John were just vendor representatives allowed to perform.

I don't want to look like a coward in my own eyes. It's my reasoned choice; it's about bravery. The very thing that Marcus Aurelius evangelizes as a stoic trait. But I'm not a Roman emperor.

Another step.

Soon, he would reach the center of the stage. What should he do? Hope for last-minute enlightenment? Risk his job and go against his company's message?

The last step.

Who was he to decide what serves Sellingpower best? There he stood, staring into a blurred wall of light. No faces. Just fear.

"Hi everyone," Elias said.

Hell, who am I to know it better?

"As John said, numbers make numbers!" Stretching out his arm towards John, he also saw Jessica shaking her head in disbelief.

I'm sorry, Jessica. I'm sorry, brave Elias.

He looked at his black shoes. He had cleaned them this morning, and there were still stains on them. Next time, he should be more careful. People judge other people by their shoes. And by how much they sweat.

Stop thinking about that! Speak. Now.

"I want to tell you a story about how numbers helped one of Sellingpower's biggest clients to become wildly successful. Their sales management team desperately needed to justify funding for new hires. To gain the respective data, they called us for a solution as…"

Suddenly, a *bang* pulled Elias out of his talk. He ducked, and the audience groaned. Then the spotlights went dark. In front of his eyes danced sparkles of light. Kneeling, he scanned the hall to see what had happened. Then he saw it: the open bottle that John had kicked off the stage lay two meters away. The water had formed a puddle, enough to seep into a transformer, shorting a circuit. A fine line of smoke rose.

Elias stood up.

Quickly, the moderator came on stage and reassured the anxious-looking audience. "Everything is under control."

Is it really? Every heartbeat hammered on Elias' guilt. *There is your sign. When the going gets tough, the tough get going.*

The lights went on again. Elias froze, his mind completely empty. He only heard the cracks of snow that his running shoes had made. Then he lifted his chin, pressed his shoulders back, and stood upright. Elias smiled the smile of a person who finally understood.

"As much as John is a charismatic person," he continued his speech, "...his message is flawed. You hear it from every vendor in our industry, not realizing that it disregards the individual contributor: the person who actually enters data into an application is core to your business."

There was no fear anymore, only relief.

Elias did the right thing. He knew that Jessica was smiling broadly.

John shook his head.

"Numbers don't make numbers. Not even your company does. Your employees do!"

54

THOUGHT LEADERS BREAK THE RULES

ELIAS SHOWED you what braveness means to him. He used his reasoned choice, his power to control the situation and do what seems right. What would you have done?

Let's crunch some more ideas around the topic.

Look at the following two statements. Which one draws your attention the most?

First, "I love my new Mac. It's so beautiful, and everything feels so smooth about it."

Second, "I would never use a Mac in my life. It's a product of a money-printing machine based on marketing fluff. I only trust Microsoft."

Typically, we humans are attracted to quarrels and like to take sides. We love to take a position and argue for it. Most likely, you are a Mac fan or a Microsoft fan, not both at the same time.

Marketing uses this human instinct as a tool to attract people's attention. In his book *This is Marketing*[1], Seth Godin makes a great point: "People like us do things like that." We want to stay with our crowd and share equal opinions with them. Those opinions may even be the holy grail for us.

The same principle applies to thought leadership. You're

standing up for a provocative opinion, and you attract everyone who agrees with you (and doesn't). Naturally, you're creating a ditch. This discord makes fans. It's at play every day: football clubs like FC Bayern München vs. Borussia Dortmund, car brands like BMW vs. Mercedes, camera brands like Nikon vs. Canon, dog lovers vs. cat lovers. Or think about the finance department's morning coffee break at Starbucks, where nobody else is allowed to join because it's their ritual.

Now you might ask, how could you apply a provocative opinion in your daily interaction with prospects?

The easiest way to do that is to start with a vision of your company and product. Is it controversial or pretty traditional? In the latter case, start chasing your product marketing management team and ask them to craft a bolder vision with you. Maybe their ideas are already spinning in your mind?

As an example, Mulesoft started in the traditional Enterprise Service Bus (ESB) market and tried to thrive for years. In 2014, they left the path of a conventional Enterprise Application Integration (EAI) patterns solution. Instead, they reinvented themselves, becoming a tool for implementing integration microservices. They invented and evangelized a new methodology for integration that overtook EAI and created a new hype by launching themselves into this new realm. Mulesoft called it 'API-led Connectivity.'

At the time, it was a bold and visionary move, absolutely unique, and it definitely confused the competition. The integration market needed some time to readjust and prepare an answer to MuleSoft's new positioning.

Some of MuleSoft's prospects didn't agree with the fancy new world of integration, but some became huge fans of their new approach—and it created two opposing camps.

Yet, the technical, architectural, and methodical positioning was not the end. Additionally, Mulesoft conceptualized an organizational model that focused on reuse and self-service in large companies. Therefore, the offering included a technical solution, a novel architecture and implementation style, and an organizational model.

Customers in the MuleSoft camp loved it because it addressed all of the pillars of change: people, process, and technology. Remember them when you formulate your message, your methodology, your vision.

Now, go and watch out for traditional rules you can break; create fans and opponents.

INSTANT CHALLENGE!

What's a set-in-stone rule in your industry? What's so common you wouldn't even dare think to change it?

Write it down here.

Then ask yourself why this change is actually a positive one. Document your reasoning below.

Under no circumstances should you share the result.

#salesengineers #breakingrules #positioning

55

SHARING MEANS CARING

Noise filled the hall, and Elias moved his weight from his right foot to his left. After finishing his presentation, he strolled over to the display area and connected his laptop at the Sellingpower booth. Thanks to him speaking, Sellingpower had got a stand at the expo. He didn't even notice that John had disappeared. A group of people strolled past him and scanned the slogans on the monitors.

"May I show you how the Sellingpower solution works?" Elias asked. He smiled and pointed towards the display.

The group of people stopped. Their red ribbons most likely meant they were PeopleLove competitors. "Sure, can you elaborate on how your AI gets trained to generate the strength profiles?"

"We'll help you assemble the data you have in-house. Then we mix that data with obfuscated information from our clients," Elias explained.

The group nodded and started to discuss something. It seemed they were in disagreement whether such an approach was ethical.

Suddenly, a well-groomed man with a tailored suit stopped in front of Elias.

"Hi. No demo needed," the man grinned. "I wanted to say that your speech was inspiring. It didn't sound like something Ralf would support, though. When did Sellingpower change its decades-old messaging?"

Oh crap, this guy knows Ralf. Did I harm Sellingpower? Elias smiled lightly, feverishly looking for a good answer. "I don't think the company did, actually."

"If you need a new challenge, please call me." The guy handed him a business card. Johan Ostred. CEO, Hubpoint. "We're growing massively, and I could use a bright person like you. I've always thought that sales engineers are the best executors of category design initiatives. You're proving my point."

"Don't tell that to marketing." Elias grinned and pounded the card on his fingers. "Let me give it a thought. Thanks a lot."

"You wouldn't need to staff a booth with my company." Johan clapped Elias' shoulder and walked away with a charismatic laugh.

Demoing software and answering questions are core to my job. But maybe it's time to leave that behind.

Suddenly, like Moses parting the Red Sea, Jessica effortlessly made her way through the crowd. As she came closer, she smiled brightly. She hugged him, making him giggle like a school child. Elias' face turned red.

"That was an excellent presentation! You had me believing that you would glorify Sellingpower's old-school messages."

"Well, to be honest…"

"The twist was amazing. But you definitely didn't need to destroy our equipment."

"Thank you, Jessica. I don't know what to say."

"I recorded your part of the speech and shared it on ConnectedOut. It's already had 50,000 views. You should know what to say soon."

What did she say? Recorded? Shared? Elias fell onto the bar chair that was in his booth. Such a huge reach frightened him.

Thoughts of the death threats against his parents came up. What if that were to happen to him now? He was upsetting a lot of people.

"Is everything alright?" Jessica asked.

He shook his head. *What would Ralf say? He must have already seen that I changed the speech. I dismissed his very clear order to stay with the old farts messaging. But hey, I stayed true to myself.*

Then he nodded and finally smiled. "I'm good."

"This was your breakthrough. You've honed your message for months, and it came across brilliantly."

"Because of your advice, Jessica. All honor to you." Elias said.

Jessica laughed. "I haven't done anything. Just sending you some direct messages. You put the work in, nobody else."

"What will Ralf say?"

"I guess he will love the success. Why do you ask?"

"Because he forced me to use the old messaging."

She seemed to understand now. "Oh!" With a serious view, she scanned him. "You might want to think about whether Sellingpower is the right company for you."

"But, I can't leave them now I did that to them." *It's like pouring water into the sauna oven just to leave afterwards.*

"Believe me; you did them a big favor. The amount of brand attention you just gave them would cost marketing several million."

Maybe she's right. I worked on it for months, and now Sellingpower has all the attention again. I don't want to go through another Tim story. Elias nodded while scanning the room. Then he spotted the guy he was looking for. Johan.

"Thanks, Jessica. Please, excuse me. I have to get a new job."

56

THOUGHT LEADERS DEAL WITH SUCCESS

ELIAS' braveness has made him famous, but he can't quite believe it. Already, new opportunities are opening up, and it would be easy for him to become arrogant. Let's hope that won't happen to him.

But what does success mean? You've already read about it being a staircase with an endless amount of steps. It seems there's no final success. There might be people who claim to have found it, but have they managed to keep it? Remember, the things you cling to will run away from you. Additionally, true success should always involve your health, friends, and family.

Let's take a look at the achievement of becoming a million-aire, for example. For a lot of people, happiness is defined as possessing an endless stream of money. What does it tell you that most lottery winners lose their wealth in a short amount of time and even find that their riches ruin their lives[1]?

One explanation is that money reinforces existing traits. It doesn't make you an evil, immoral person. But if you've been greedy, unfair, and envious for your whole life, having more money will likely intensify those behaviors. On the other hand, people who have found happiness in themselves have learned not to compare themselves to others. They regularly donate money and take the creation of sense and purpose into their own hands, meaning they will be more likely to grow those traits in the case of a full bank account.

But you should also watch yourself. Is there arrogance creeping along like a shadow with every successful step you take? Are you objectively observing yourself? Do you still network with the people you regarded as equal before you had success? Do you brag? Do you gossip?

Find a mantra to stay on track and not to slip into bad behavior. You could tell yourself that you want to be known for doing good and not for living an extraordinary and luxurious life. You could be known for spending on people and not on your reputation.

Have you heard of José Mujica[2]? "El Pepe" served as the 40th president of Uruguay from 2010 to 2015. He earned $12,000 a month in his roles and donated 90% of that to charities[3] supporting poor people and small entrepreneurs.

Be that inspiring person yourself. Donate regularly!

Take 10% of what you earn monthly and give it back. No matter how low your income might feel today, just start. Once you are successful, it might feel tough to donate 10% because your lifestyle sucks the money up. So let the absolute amount of donation grow with your success.

This principle truly changes the world for good. You will make a difference that way, and you will be dealing with your success like a humble leader.

INSTANT CHALLENGE!

Scribble down three causes you would like to donate to, for example:

- saving oceans,
- or the rainforest,
- education,
- or supporting the world's poorest children.

Then donate. Do it now, even if it's a small amount of money, like $3. It's just the price of a coffee, but it will help.

Share that you donated with your network. We shouldn't be shy about it because we don't want others to feel shy about it. Donation is important; giving back for our lucky lifestyle is a simple matter of gratitude.

#salesengineers #doinggood #givingback

57

THE INTERVIEW

"As far as I understand, your presentation annoyed some people a lot." Johan leaned over the table to grab some bread and dipped it into the luxury olive oil. He chewed and smiled at Elias. "But deep in his heart, Ralf knew that it was about time for a change."

Elias found himself in a cold restaurant that contrasted his usual cozy teahouse both in mood and temperature. He wrapped his hands around his coffee cup. Then he took a sip. Much too bitter for his taste. "Tell me about Hubpoint. Why am I here?"

Johan shrugged. "You remind me of myself. I worked as a sales engineer at a software company before founding Hubpoint."

"So we did the same job. That's the reason?"

"In my day, we competed against the big guys with a shiny and small but valuable solution. In terms of features, we weren't competitive at all."

"Having too few features is definitely not one of Sellingpower's concerns." Elias rolled his eyes and shook his head. "A customer-created configuration monster."

Johan nodded, then continued his story. "But we started to dominate our niche in a big way. So big that we spilled over into greater niches where features became essential to winning clients. Things got tough outside our category, but we needed to keep the money flowing in. So we competed."

"And today, you know you should have done things differently? Is this where the story is going?"

"Well, one rainy day, I sat with a prospect who invited us because of our niche capabilities. Actually, it became obvious that he misunderstood what we did. The prospect had formed a so-called anti-agile team and wanted our software to support it. That day, I had a revelation. The idea that this guy would complement our product perfectly and allow us to not only sell tech but also…"

"A novel methodology."

"Exactly. Including the required organizational change."

Elias nodded. *How does Herbert express it?* "Technology alone doesn't make any client successful."

"Bingo," Johan smiled. "A change of habit is needed for an organization to find a new pattern of working."

"And then your company offered that, and you succeeded?"

"Well, I started working out a concept for a new offering to pitch to the product team. It seemed promising because the CEO also joined the meeting."

"An epic meeting of stones."

Johan looked at Elias sideways and had question marks in his eyes.

"Sorry. I heard this from a soccer coach a while back. He wanted players to be sponges, not stones. Growth mindset people."

"Oh, in this case. Yes, I spoke to stones. But I didn't give up that quickly and got an account executive on my side. We worked on a strategic prospect. I convinced him to pitch the anti-agile team solution under the radar of our management. So we created a compelling deck that included the product and a roadmap of organizational change. The message went viral, and soon our prospect's CEO wanted to speak to my CEO."

"That must have been a meeting full of tension."

"We were on the edge of closing the strategic deal, and our CEO was pitched by our prospect on what a great job we'd done. He had no choice but to follow our lead. We literally added an organizational approach to our technology because the market desired it."

"I hope things went more smoothly from then on."

"Sure, product management, sales engineers, and professional services got together to work out a strategy. Everybody was excited by the opportunity."

"Everybody?"

Elias and Johan laughed loudly.

"Well, some people left. I found myself speaking at a Gartner event some weeks later about how a product-led growth strategy isn't enough in our digital age. A truly transformational offering needs to cover people, process, and technology." Johan pointed with another piece of bread towards Elias. "And? Does that sound familiar to you?"

"Yes. I guess so. Even from outside Hubpoint, I can see your principles at work. What happened to your co-founder, by the way?" Elias asked.

"He left because he insisted on donating 15% of our income every month. As much as I get the philanthropic idea, it was simply too much money."

Elias didn't know what to say and tried another sip of coffee. The worst one he'd had for a long time, and maybe the most expensive. "I need to invite you to my favorite teahouse."

Johan watched Elias for a while, dipped some more bread into the oil, and asked, "Can I count you in?"

"On my teahouse invitation? Sure!" Elias looked the CEO straight in the eyes.

Johan laughed; his piece of bread landed on his plate and fell onto the table. "No, man. I want you to work for me."

"Are you kidding? Of course! You already got me when you said how I annoyed some people. I'm free in two months."

"You have until Friday."

58

THOUGHT LEADERS THINK

Elias has started thinking about business and the inner workings of sales in broader terms. He has grown his skills and can now use them to speak on the same level as executives. That wouldn't have happened without the challenges he had to overcome. He's been thinking.

But we all think, don't we? Just read on to find out.

International Business Machines (IBM) is one of the oldest tech companies on the planet. It nearly died in 1993 but managed to recover[1]. If you've ever worked at IBM or know someone who has, you will have noticed their five-letter slogan: *Think!*

Thomas J. Watson said in 1911 that, "The trouble with every one of us is that we don't think enough. We don't get paid for working with our feet—we get paid for working with our heads."

This statement is still true today.

And for us as sales engineers with a queue flooded with opportunities to work on, we must think about how to prioritize them. We must think about how to free up time to think about our job—why we do it and how to improve it for everyone else in the domain.

It's wise to invest time in finding out what helps you think. Not just the fast, associative way of thinking that Kahneman describes in *Thinking Fast and Slow* but also the method that Nicholas Taleb suggests in *Black Swan*: long, contemplative walks. André Kostolany[2], a famous stock speculator, preferred sitting and spending time on deep thinking.

What is the right way? There isn't one. One practical method is to use your associative brain to come up with lots of ideas. It can spit out several ideas on any given topic in minutes. With those in your hands, have a stroll through your neighborhood and add some substance to them. You might also want to let your unconscious work by sitting and doing nothing.

This method is called idea storming. And all you need is a pen and paper. Assign yourself the task of developing fifteen ideas on how to improve your daily sales engineering work. Then, off you go!

Only one line per idea is allowed. Be concise; be open, and permit ideas that aren't good. What's important here is that you tell your brain to let it come. No judgment. Done daily, this will improve your idea generation.

With that list, you can now start thinking deeply about a topic that resonates with you. Then, walk for an hour and think about that topic. Contemplative walking is a powerful concept. But walk slowly. Actually, walk so slowly that you forget you're walking at all. It's not about fitness; it's about creating a state of flow or even meditation.

The reality is that our minds are overwhelmed with issues on our agenda—things we need to get done. If you struggle with this, you can make your muddy brain-water clear by practicing meditation. You will make your contemplative walks more successful if you've trained your mind to concentrate by meditating. Don't know where to start? Sign up for an app; there are plenty out there.

And then think like you haven't thought before!

INSTANT CHALLENGE!

Put this book in your pocket, lace your shoes, set a timer for thirty minutes, and just stroll. Once the timer rings, take a photo of yourself and the book. Then walk back.

At home, publish the picture with a description of what you experienced.

#salesengineers #innovation #habits

59

ALL HANDS ON DECK, YEAH!

THE SELLINGPOWER MEETING room was crowded. Everyone had heard about Elias' keynote and the buzz it had caused in the CRM market (although the idea of the CRM empowering individual contributors instead of managers seemed to confuse parts of the organization.)

On top of that, Sarah and Herbert had closed a five-year strategic partnership with PeopleLove, championed by Jessica.

Elias scanned the room. Only about twenty people were physically present: Maria, Sarah, professional services, and customer success colleagues. The remaining 250 attendees were watching remotely.

Ralf stood in front of the crowd, looking into a professional camera mounted behind them, blocking the yellow fridge. Elias would have loved to have grabbed a lemonade.

Ralf placed his hand on his chest. "If you are as old as I am, then you know the song 'Wind of Change.' Although I don't play the balalaika, we need to sing a new message into the market. And I want you all to sing it too."

Maria leaned forward towards Ralf and whispered something.

Nodding, Ralf said, "Thanks to the video that is currently

going viral as you young folks tend to say, we are changing direction with our marketing and product team. Headquarters approved it yesterday night."

There was a strange mood in the room. Everybody stayed quiet and passive. Elias peeked around him but couldn't find anybody smiling. In addition, most of the video feeds in the online meeting remained dark, just displaying a name or avatar picture.

Elias had forced a corporation to act on his stunt at the PeopleLove conference—even managers and peers who were believed to rank higher in the food chain. They had no chance but to face the wind of change.

The pushback isn't about the new message but about the guy who brought it into existence.

Sellingpower wasn't the right company for Elias, and he was glad that he would soon be joining Hubpoint. However, nobody wanted him to explain the new message because everybody was shooting new ideas to stake a claim, to be able to shape the change. There was a fight going on, deep in the underground of the company culture. Enemies old and new seemed to spot an opportunity.

"Okay, that's all for now. We'll be sending out a briefing and messaging document this evening. Read it, own it, use it by tomorrow," Ralf said.

Suddenly, the chat was flooded with complaints about ongoing customer engagements: how to behave, customer implementations, and whether they should be stopped or course-corrected. At first, it seemed like Ralf was about to ignore them, but then he sighed and said, "Boys and girls, use common sense in existing engagements."

AFTER THE ALL-HANDS CALL, Elias stayed in the kitchen, working through some comments on ConnectedOut. Then, closing his laptop, he realized that he was alone with Maria.

He showed a fake smile and dried his wet palms on his trousers. "How are you with this?" he asked her. She looked up at him, put on a smile, and focused on her laptop again. "Good, Elias. Good."

"I really don't want any bad blood between us. We've known each other for how long? Five years?"

"Don't worry."

"Alright, but if there's anything I can do for you, please tell me."

With that, Elias went to leave for his appointment. He was going to hand in his notice to Ralf.

"You know what? There is something," she said, suddenly and amiably.

Elias stopped and gave her his full presence, waiting for what she was about to say.

"I promise you; I will ruin your life like you ruined mine. I never was, and never will be, your friend. I've hated you since day one, and I will do everything in my power to make your life hell."

Frozen, Elias stared at her. A cracking noise filled the room as his laptop hit the floor. Maria's soul-crushing candor took him completely off-guard.

His head heated like an oven plate as he bent down to grab his laptop. To avoid looking into Maria's eyes, he turned the device around and inspected it from every angle. It broke open on one edge and the display showed a spiderweb.

"I understand your frustration, Maria. I am sorry for you."

"You suck!"

Elias nodded. With a grave face, he walked out of the room towards Ralf's office. There was a whirlwind in his head, his thoughts being blown around like leaves.

Why does she hate me so much? What have I done to her?

Looking out of his office window, Ralf peeled a banana as Elias entered the room. "Close the door, please."

Elias turned around and gave it a bump with his foot.

Ralf took a bite and faced his visitor. "Did you leave your laptop on the street?" Ralf asked.

"What?" Elias had nearly forgotten the broken device. "No, Maria was just seriously honest with me, and I'm still confused."

"What's that got to do with your laptop?"

Elias shrugged his shoulders, trying to look innocent.

"Maria has been fired. Partly because of your stunt."

"So, you're blaming me, too?"

"You changed a lot for us. Actually, *I can* see the opportunity in this. Our inbound leads have gone up by 2300% over the last two days."

Elias' chair squeaked as he fell into it. "Wow."

"Well, most of the prospects want to speak with you." Ralf smiled. "You might be our next bottleneck."

Elias could hardly gulp. How could he tell Ralf that he was leaving Sellingpower to work for Hubpoint?

"No worries." Ralf stood up and rested on the edge of his table, looking down at Elias. "You'll get two weeks to assemble enablement material for your colleagues."

Elias didn't move a muscle. He stared out of the window.

Ralf inspected his clothing. "Do I have a spot on my shirt?"

Now or never.

"I'm leaving Sellingpower." The sentence sounded shallow, so Elias cleared his throat. He sucked in air and pushed it out forcefully. "Friday will be my last day, Ralf."

60

THOUGHT LEADERS ARE CONSTANT LEARNERS

Elias doesn't stand still. He feels that there's no more he will learn when staying with Sellingpower. What would you do in his situation? Stay?

There are different types of thought leaders.

You might be a thought-leading sales engineer with a fixed opinion that is strongly informative and based on experience and reputation.

Or you might use a provocative point of view, fighting the status quo and proposing non-traditional approaches to solve industry problems.

Then again, you might be a product or industry expert sharing best practices, how-tos, training, or the hottest news on the topic.

You have to decide which path to follow. It needs to fit your personality, or preferably, the personality you want to become. Nobody ever reached their limit; there's always space to grow. Don't stop; train every day; grow. If you have read this far, you have most likely accepted that lifelong challenge, and you may already have set your next goal.

Staying motivated to push forward constantly depends on

your curiosity. How much knowledge are you willing to inhale daily? It's one thing to dive deep into your area of expertise; that might come easily to you, and you will certainly have the feeling you can't learn everything in one lifetime. But it's crucial that you cross-read into domains that are adjacent and even independent of yours. Like a good retirement stock portfolio—diversify.

The brain is a beautiful pattern-detection instrument that will help you draw analogies between your area of expertise and an unrelated topic. This will level up your publications, making them unique and original. It may even lead to a new way of looking at your industry.

A historical example comes from the quantum scientist Paul Dirac[1]. He was a key player in the development of quantum mechanics theory, but he had an engineering background, unlike any other contemporary theoretical physicist. Therefore, he felt very comfortable using technical drawings. He used them to understand quantum concepts, and if he found a solution this way, he rewrote them into beautiful mathematical equations.

His approach was unique, and he found elegant solutions that were not accessible to others.

The author of the book in your hand isn't Paul Dirac. Still, you might have realized the mix of a fictional story, philosophical principles, and brand building. Yet another merge—combining sales engineering and fantasy novels—led to the sales engineering software application market fantasy map (see the image below.) The idea for the map didn't come naturally, but after a long walk before a webinar. The map's creator thought about how best to visualize the core message for the upcoming presentation. It's serendipity that he is a fantasy author who tried the newest map drawing tool for a novel and applied it to the domain of sales engineering.

The map is still developing, and you can find the newest version at salesengineeringmap.com.

So, keep walking, stealing, mixing, creating, and *learning*! Serendipity hangs about everywhere.

INSTANT CHALLENGE!

What's your next goal? It's a tough question, which is why you should come up with five different answers quickly. Highlight the one that resonates strongly with you.

Now, plan what knowledge and routine you need to achieve that very goal.

Enjoy.

And don't forget to post about it.

#salesengineers #dailyroutine #goals

61

THE LEGAL STUFF

FOR SIX WEEKS, Elias worked as the community evangelist for AI at Hubpoint. It took him four weeks to come to an agreement with Johan on the new messaging. So far, it hadn't taken off in the market; the timespan was simply too short. Even the growth-hacking initiatives that allowed subscribers to gift quarterly premium access to their customers hadn't been successful.

In a David-and-Goliath-style fight, Hubpoint planned to beat Sellingpower, and they had everything they needed except patience. It didn't go as smoothly as Elias had wished for; the message seemed forced, and Johan didn't allow enough time for it to evolve. Months ago at Sellingpower, Elias had played it relaxed, shaping the punchline a little bit every day. But there hadn't been a job to lose then. Now there was.

He prayed for Johan to show more patience or to have his messaging prove its magic powers. Like a puzzle piece forced into the wrong position, he didn't feel his natural fit for the organization. Still, Elias didn't want to give up on the task, so he waited for a genius idea to hit him. That's why he stayed at Hubpoint: hope.

WHILE THIS WAS HAPPENING, Sellingpower hadn't given up on him.

One morning, Elias carried an unwelcome message into Johan's office.

"They did *what?*" the Hubpoint CEO shouted. His huge office window gave a panoramic view of London. The weather was as foggy as Elias' mood.

"They claim that I'm legally not allowed to work for you," Elias repeated, showing Johan the piece of paper he'd received from a Sellingpower lawyer. "My role as community evangelist for AI is too close to my previous position."

"This is nonsense. I'll talk to Bertrand. He'll fight you out of this." With stiff fingers, Johan typed something into his smartphone.

Should I tell him Jessica's news? The whole Hubpoint stunt was fun at the beginning, but now it's turning into a toxic rose war. For what? An impressive salary?

There wasn't anybody Elias wanted to impress. Actually, he dreamt of reducing his working hours because he'd found a person who enriched his life. She acknowledged him, and he wanted to spend as much time as possible with her.

Elias dreamed away to the green wallpaper of his favorite teahouse, where they would meet later.

"Done." Johan threw his phone on his massive office desk. "We'll get Sellingpower in front of the court. They can't do that to you." Then he lay his hand on Elias' shoulder. "Don't worry about it."

"Can't we just ignore it? There are other things I can work on."

"That would mean me losing you as my community-building spearhead! Are you crazy?"

"Your team got the message. They inhaled it. I shouldn't be needed."

"If you say that again, I will fire you." Johan put on his charming smile. Long wrinkles around his eyes turned him back into the sympathetic leader Elias met some months ago. Yet, there appeared to be some cracks in the facade because of the CEO's huge ego.

"I'm not needed, Johan," Elias said.

Hubpoint's CEO stood still as the smile melted from his face. The realization that Elias was serious seemed to have struck him.

"And I thought you were loyal!"

Elias had feared Johan would say that. And although he considered himself to be a person with integrity, that didn't mean he wanted to fight other people's wars. Too many things were going on that were outside his control. Indeed, it wasn't the job that he'd started six weeks ago, and this company would be a different one pretty soon.

"Sellingpower will buy you out!" At least Elias wanted to be honest with Johan. Jessica had told him this news in private.

Johan pressed long arms against the window and let his head fall between his shoulders. "I saw that coming. They've already bought 20% of our shares."

"What can you do to counter their attack?"

"Not much. They want us to execute on your original message, don't they?"

"It's not mine. It evolved too much. I'm not the owner of that marketing statement anymore."

Elias had followed the stock market. Sellingpower had nearly tripled in price since he'd left and climbed the ladder to the undisputed CRM champion. He didn't think the takeover was to get him back; it was simply to employ more execution power on the ground. Hubpoint was the perfect candidate to grow Sellingpower's workforce.

"What is it that you want? More money? More equity? No problem." Johan observed Elias' face. As he wasn't answering,

Johan continued. "Okay, 250k per year and an additional 10k of stock options."

Elias felt the urge to swallow the bait. That was more money than he had ever dreamed of. Such prosperity was unknown in his family. But was that for a reason, maybe? Elias grew up with his grandparents after his mother and father fled. Before his death, Elias' grandfather said he didn't want to be a slave, even if that meant never eating with golden spoons.

Then there were Jessica's lectures about Seneca, who said that the only thing under control is your reasoned choice. Nothing else. Not even your body—and certainly no amount of money.

But somehow, I enjoy working with Johan. We've already shaped the market a bit; we are working on a strategy to overcome Selling-power's dominance. It could work if Hubpoint doesn't get bought out beforehand.

Elias shook his head while looking Johan in the eye. His mouth was dry when he continued. "My strategy for life has changed. I will be a free man like you are."

Johan had watched Elias all the time. Now, he nodded and said, "It was an honor, Elias."

62

THOUGHT LEADERS UNDERSTAND
THE DIFFERENCE BETWEEN
STRATEGY AND TACTIC

ELIAS DECIDES against a big opportunity because it doesn't fit into his strategy for life.

A strategy is a long-term plan to reach your bigger goals. Tactics, on the other hand, are the short-term actions that support it.

Your non-job-related strategy could be to marry the person you fell in love with two years ago. Your tactics might be to offer friendship, ask the person out on a date, and become acquainted with their parents.

Many tactics usually support one strategy.

But how are strategy and tactics different? Tactics change frequently, and you need them to be flexible. Sometimes, people just imitate the tactics of others, be it style, processes, content, or visualization (such as doing comic-like doodly explainer videos to attract customers; do you remember the short-term hype around them?)

Most tactics are pleasing as long as they work. When the hype is over, the person who *intentionally* used explainer videos as a tactic to achieve a greater outcome will be off implementing a new tactic while you still fiddle around learning it and are left puzzled when it doesn't bring in the results you expected.

The person who didn't have a strategy at all will be left beaten up, wondering where all the other people went.

As a thought leader, you should develop and follow your personal strategy. For example, you could derive a blueprint from the indie book publishing book industry. The strategy would be to build an empire of fans who you can reach via your platform. The important words in the previous sentence are *your* and *platform*.

You don't control your followers and content when you rely on a third-party social media app or retailer. Platforms you do own are a newsletter, an app, a forum, or your website's membership area, depending on your IT skills and your appetite for spending.

No matter how your platform looks, your strategy is to collect all those people who love your work and original thinking. That way, whatever happens to the most popular social business or networking app of your time, you can still reach your fans.

So there's your strategy: build a platform that you own. Make it crowded with your fans so you can reach out whenever you want to offer them your articles, courses, challenges, books, videos, or whatever gimmick allows you to express yourself. You can also consider growing this into the small kingdom that enables you to live as free as you want.

Becoming independent from an employer can also be a strategy. Reaching thought leader status could be a tactic in that greater scheme.

You get the point.

On your thought leadership journey, it's important to understand that using the hippest, shiniest platform—that you don't own—is merely a tactic. Ensure you know why you are servicing the hype app, and employ a way to dispatch people towards your kingdom consistently. In other words, use it as a funnel.

Tactics are vast and will differ with trends in tech and people's tastes. Sometimes, it's just needed to prospect fans by sending them a message directly. Sometimes, you need bait to convince them to settle in your kingdom. Maybe you set up a recommendation service for niche books or run challenges addressing the audience that fits your thought leadership area.

You will achieve the best level of familiarity with your target audience when serving them with regular specific content both on your platform and a mass platform. And if you need a bigger funnel, you just increase the number of services and networks you upload your content to—but ensure that every new follower gets the chance to join your platform.

In summary, your strategy should be to **build your kingdom**.

Do it with whatever tactic works at the time, and be prepared to deploy a new one at a moment's notice.

True success doesn't come through your fame but through the constant building of your platform. Small daily habits and increments of followers are enough to achieve that in the long run. It's not a sprint if you want reliable results.

One day, your efforts will send echos back to you in the manifestation of a speaking engagement, an advisory board seat, options in a startup, your own company, or complete independence.

INSTANT CHALLENGE!

Revisit your biggest goal from the last challenge. Now think about a strategy for how you could achieve it. Follow up with tactics to implement your strategy and bring your goal to life.

First, list your strategy.

Second, list five tactics that would support it.

And…well, you know the drill.

#salesengineers #socialselling #career

63

HE WHO KNOWS EVERYTHING

IT WAS a sunny afternoon when Ralf drove into the old castle's parking space. A lot of other guests had parked their cars and were walking towards the ceremony hall. He followed them and wished his wife could have found the time to join him.

Hopefully, I'll know at least a few people here.

In the entrance was a seating plan that assigned numbers to guests. Ralf smiled cheekily.

Is that Elias' way of being ironic?

Then he found his name and approached table four. With relief, he saw Maria sitting there. Ralf greeted her with a smile as he sat down at the colossal table decorated with flowers and candles.

"Nice to see you, Maria. I wouldn't have expected to meet you here."

She blushed. "Well, me neither. But Elias sent me such a lovely invitation that I couldn't resist."

"Do you want to tell me?" Ralf asked as he took a sip of the Prosecco he'd been handed by an attentive waiter.

"I needed to think about the meaning for a while, to be honest." She toasted towards Ralf and drank.

"Don't keep me in suspense. What jumped out of his creative mind?"

Maria giggled. "I don't think it would resonate with a sales guy."

"No worries, Maria. I left Sellingpower, and I work on my wife's farm now. That's why she can't be here. She rescued two horses from the slaughterhouse today. You could say that I'm a farmer now."

"That sounds amazing. And a bit strange."

Ralf was caught by his thoughts for a moment and then said: "Well, as far as I understand, the bridal couple will donate every penny they get from us to an ocean-cleaning charity."

"I was impressed when I first heard that. Had I known that Elias is such a deeply caring person, I would have treated him differently."

Ralf nodded and smiled. "What about you?"

"I'm happy at a startup that produces underwear for plus-size men. Technology isn't my area of expertise. I guess that's what I learned from Elias."

"I'm glad for you." Ralf scanned the hall. Close to the table of the bridal couple was a dancing area. Behind it, a DJ was finalizing his setup. There he saw Sarah and Herbert chatting and laughing. He knew that both were still at Sellingpower. Sarah had been promoted to VP of sales, taking Ralf's position. Herbert led a team of sales engineers who focused on value selling.

"We built a great company with Sellingpower, Maria. It was a pleasure to have worked with you. But I recognize that it ended badly."

"No worries. If it hadn't, I would still be unhappy. My attitude was poisonous; I know that now."

"This must be the old colleague's table!" said Herbert as he pushed Sarah's chair forward as she sat down.

"Hallo, Herbert. Es ist schön, dich zu sehen."

"Thanks, Ralf. Your German skills are excellent."

Maria cleared her throat. "Does anybody actually know what Elias is doing now? I heard he left Hubpoint after the announcement of the Sellingpower acquisition."

Herbert looked at everyone and said, "I know because I'm his client. He founded a company that helps sales engineers build their brands. And he fights for them to become monetized for their network and influence."

"So Sellingpower pays you for posting?" Ralf asked.

"Absolutely!" Herbert's smile wandered up to his eyes.

"And what about Jessica?" Ralf wanted to know.

"She's still at PeopleLove but on maternity leave," Sarah said and looked at Herbert.

Suddenly, wedding music played and filled the hall. Everybody watched the entry. And then, the bride appeared. Jessica wore an elegant ivory wedding dress. Elias walked proudly at her side.

"The smoking jacket suits him," said Herbert to Ralf. "I should get one myself."

Ralf enjoyed the wedding and meeting his old colleagues. He could still sympathize with his past and the great people he had the chance to work with.

Later that evening, he picked up the conversation with Maria. "So, what did Elias write on the invitation?"

Maria silently looked at Ralf for quite a while before she answered, "He who knows everything, forgives everything."

FINAL INSTANT CHALLENGE!

Thanks so much, dear reader.

If you've followed Elias this far, you may feel motivated to go on your own journey. And I can only tell you that it's worth it. Please, get back to me with your experiences. I look forward to hearing from you.

And here comes your last challenge:

Hit Amazon and leave a review of this book. Then post it on your social media account. For your karma.

#salesengineers #karma #bookreview

APPENDIX: FURTHER READING

1. Maney, Kevin., Peterson, Dave., Ramadan, Al., Lochhead, Christopher. Play Bigger: *How Rebels and Innovators Create New Categories and Dominate Markets.* United Kingdom: Piatkus, 2016.
2. Trout, Jack., Ries, Al. *The 22 Immutable Laws of Marketing.* United Kingdom: HarperCollins, 1994.
3. Kleon, Austin. *Steal Like an Artist: 10 Things Nobody Told You About Being Creative.* United States: Workman Publishing Company, 2012.
4. Salz, Lee B.. *Sales Differentiation: 19 Powerful Strategies to Win More Deals at the Prices You Want.* United States: AMACOM, 2018.
5. Taleb, Nassim Nicholas. *The Black Swan: Second Edition: The Impact of the Highly Improbable Fragility".* United States: Random House Publishing Group, 2010.
6. Kruse, Peter. *next practice: Erfolgreiches Management von Instabilität. Veränderung durch Vernetzung.* Germany: GABAL Verlag GmbH, 2020.
7. Anderson, Chris. 2017. *TED talks: the official TED guide to public speaking.* Boston: MIfflin Harcourt,

2017.

8. Carnegie, Dale. *The Art of Public Speaking: The Original Tool for Improving Public Oration.* United States: Clydesdale, 2018.

9. Godin, Seth. *This Is Marketing: You Can't Be Seen Until You Learn to See.* United States: Penguin Publishing Group, 2018.

10. Holiday, Ryan, Hanselman, Stephen. *The Daily Stoic: 366 Meditations on Wisdom, Perseverance, and the Art of Living.* United States: Portfolio/Penguin, 2016.

11. Mandino, Og. *The Greatest Salesman in the World.* United States: F. Fell, 1983.

12. DeMarco, M. J.. *Unscripted: Life, Liberty, and the Pursuit of Entrepreneurship.* United States: Viperion Publishing Corporation, 2017.

13. Covey, Stephen R.. *The 7 Habits of Highly Effective People: 30th Anniversary Edition.* United States: Simon & Schuster, 2020.

14. Riefstahl, Robert. *Demonstrating to Win! The Indispensable Guide for Demonstrating Complex Products.* United States: Demonstrating to Win!, 2011.

15. White, Chris. *The Six Habits of Highly Effective Sales Engineers.* N.p.: Amazon Digital Services LLC - KDP Print US, 2019.

16. Care, John, Bohlig, Aron. *Mastering Technical Sales: The Sales Engineer's Handbook.* United States: Artech House, 2014.

17. Pissang, Patrick. *The Subtle Art of Sales Engineering.* Independently Published, 2020.

18. Pissang, Patrick. *Sales Engineering Exposed.* ZEMP Golden Goose GmbH, 2021.

19. Schwarzenegger, Arnold. *Total Recall: My Unbelievably True Life Story.* Waterville, Maine: Thorndike Press, 2012.

NOTES

1. Foreword

1. Ewan Clayton, "Where did writing begin?" *British Library*, accessed September 1, 2021, https://www.bl.uk/history-of-writing/articles/where-did-writing-begin#.

2. Introduction, or how to put wood into the oven

1. Hal Gregersen, *Questions are the Answer* (Harper Business, 2018), 128-129.
2. Neil Patel, "The Psychology of Instant Gratification and How It Will Revolutionize Your Marketing Approach" *Entrepreneur.Europe*, accessed September 1, 2021, https://www.entrepreneur.com/article/235088.

4. Thought leaders find meaning (in philosophy)

1. "Seneca the Younger," *Wikipedia*, accessed September 1, 2021, https://en.wikipedia.org/wiki/Seneca_the_Younger.

6. Thought leaders went through the threshold

1. "Hero's journey," *Wikipedia*, accessed September 1, 2021, https://en.wikipedia.org/wiki/Hero%27s_journey.
2. "Joseph Campbell," *Wikipedia*, accessed September 1, 2021 https://en.wikipedia.org/wiki/Joseph_Campbell.
3. "Christopher Vogler," *Wikipedia*, accessed September 1, 2021 https://en.wikipedia.org/wiki/Christopher_Vogler.

10. Thought leaders talk about problem-solving, not features

1. "Category Design," *Wikipedia*, accessed September 1, 2021, https://en.wikipedia.org/wiki/Category_design.
2. "Salesforce," *Wikipedia*, accessed September 1, 2021, https://en.wikipedia.org/wiki/Salesforce.

14. Thoughts against your online presence as a thought leader

1. Chris Voss, *Never Split the Difference: Negotiating as if Your Life Depended on It* (VOSS/RAZ, 2017).
2. Jack Nasher, *Convinced!: How to Prove Your Competence & Win People Over* (Berrett-Koehler Publishers, 2018).
3. Leslie K. John, "Savvy Self-Promotion: The delicate art, and science, of bragging," *Harvard Business Review*, May-Jun (2021), 145-148.

16. Thought leaders see opportunities in obstacles

1. »About,« *JK Rowling*, accessed September 1, 2021, https://www.jkrowling.com/about/.
2. Shay Rowbottom, "If you don't know these updates," *LinkedIn*, August, 2021, https://www.linkedin.com/posts/shayrowbottom_shayshine-linkedintips-activity-6825511426258452480-TMqI.

18. Thought leaders have a coach

1. "Live Your Best Life Using Your Strengths," *Gallup*, accessed September 1, 2021, https://www.gallup.com/cliftonstrengths/en/home.aspx.

20. Thought leaders are independent of other people's opinions

1. James Altucher, "The best writing advice I've ever received," *Medium.com*, accessed September 1, 2021, https://jaltucher.medium.com/the-best-writing-advice-ive-ever-received-449c80652350.
2. Stephen R. Covey, "Interdependence is a choice only independent people can make", *goodreads*, accessed September 1, 2021, https://www.goodreads.com/quotes/724402-interdependence-is-a-choice-only-independent-people-can-make.
3. Gregersen, *Questions Are The Answer*.

22. Thought leaders enjoy the art of stealing

1. Walter Isaacson, "The Inspiration Behind Leonardo da Vinci's Vitruvian Man," *Medium.com*, accessed September 1, 2021 https://medium.com/s/leonardo-da-vinci/the-inspiration-behind-leonardo-da-vincis-vitruvian-man-974c525495ec.

2. Austin Kleon, *Steal Like An Artist* (Workman Publishing, 2012).
3. "Albert Einstein," Wikipedia, accessed September 1, 2021, https://en.wiki pedia.org/wiki/Albert_Einstein.
4. "Niels Bohr," Wikipedia, accessed September 1, 2021, https://en.wikipedia.org/wiki/Niels_Bohr.
5. "Rutherford model," Wikipedia, accessed September 1, 2021, https://en.wikipedia.org/wiki/Rutherford_model.

28. Thought leaders build their writing craft

1. Ernest Hemingway, "The first draft of anything is shit", *goodreads*, accessed September 1, 2021, https://www.goodreads.com/quotes/52073-the-first-draft-of-anything-is-shit.

Instant challenge!

1. Based on the exercise from the book: Sol Stein, *Stein On Writing* (St. Martin's Griffin, 2000).

30. Thought leaders love black swans

1. Nassim Nicholas Taleb, *Black Swan* (Random House Publishing Group, 2010).
2. "The best software applications for Sales Engineers on a fantastic map," accessed September 1, 2021, https://salesengineeringmap.com.

32. Thought leaders understand why people follow leaders

1. From the book: Peter Kruse, *next practice: Erfolgreiches Management von Instabilität* (GABAL, 2020).
2. "Christopher Columbus," *Wikipedia*, accessed September 1, 2021, https://en.wikipedia.org/wiki/Christopher_Columbus.
3. "James Clerk Maxwell," *Wikipedia*, accessed September 1, 2021, https://en.wikipedia.org/wiki/James_Clerk_Maxwell.
4. "Michael Faraday," *Wikipedia*, accessed September 1, 2021, https://en.wiki pedia.org/wiki/Michael_Faraday.

36. Thought leaders write for the love of it

1. "some-who-will-love-it-audience", *stolen like an artist from one of James Altucher's newsletters*, https://jamesaltucher.com/.

38. Thought leaders change the culture

1. Peter Kruse, *next practice: Erfolgreiches Management von Instabilität. Veränderung durch Vernetzung* (GABAL, 2020).

40. Thought leaders stroll

1. In Ryan Holiday's *Daily Stoic*, this quote is attributed to Friedrich Nietzsche.

44. Thought leaders see competition as a stepping stone

1. Vaughn Vernon, *Implementing Domain-Driven Design* (Addison-Wesley Professional, 2013).
2. Alberto Brandolini, "Strategic Domain Driven Design with Context Mapping," *Infoq.com*, accessed September 1, 2021, https://www.infoq.com/articles/ddd-contextmapping/.
3. "DFour: Strategic Discovery using Domain-Driven Design", *saleshero.training*, https://saleshero.training/strategic-discovery-using-domain-driven-design.
4. "Rocky Balboa," *Wikipedia*, accessed September 1, 2021, https://en.wikipedia.org/wiki/Rocky_Balboa.

46. Thought leaders create their own category

1. "The best software applications for Sales Engineers on a fantastic map," accessed September 1, 2021, https://salesengineeringmap.com.
2. "Why We Launched the First Sales Experience Platform," *Walnut*, accessed September 1, 2021, https://www.walnut.io/post/why-first-sales-experience-platform-how-it-works.
3. Yoav Vilner, *LinkedIn*, accessed September 1, 2021, https://www.linkedin.com/in/yoav-vilner/.
4. Dina Brandt, *LinkedIn*, accessed September 1, 2021, https://www.linkedin.com/in/dina-brandt-trotziger-millennial/.
5. Al Ramadan et al., *Play Bigger: How Rebels and Innovators Create New Categories and Dominate Markets (Piatkus, 2016)*, 19.

48. Thought leaders lead and inspire others

1. Johann Wolfgang von Goethe, "Treat people as if they were what they ought to be and you help them to become what they are capable of being." *goodreads*, accessed September 1, 2021, https://www.goodreads.com/quotes/419209-treat-people-as-if-they-were-what-they-ought-to

50. Thought leaders understand creative disturbance

1. Oguz A. Acar, et al., "Why Constraints Are Good for Innovation", *Harvard Business Review*, accessed September 1, 2021, https://hbr.org/2019/11/why-constraints-are-good-for-innovation
2. Peter Kruse, *next practice*, 153
3. Term by Peter Kruse, *next practice*

52. Thought leaders are mentally prepared for battles

1. Ray Dalio, *Principles: Life and Work* (Simon & Schuster, 2017).
2. "Memento mori," Wikipedia, accessed September 1, 2021, https://en.wikipedia.org/wiki/Memento_mori
3. "Amor fati," Wikipedia, accessed September 1, 2021, https://en.wikipedia.org/wiki/Amor_fati
4. Ryan Holiday, *The Obstacle Is the Way: The Timeless Art of Turning Trials into Triumph* (Portfolio, 2014).

54. Thought leaders break the rules

1. Seth Godin, *This is Marketing: You Can't Be Seen Until You Learn To See* (Portfolio Penguin, 2018).

56. Thought leaders deal with success

1. Mark Abadi, "20 lottery winners who lost every penny," *Insider*, accessed September 1, 2021, https://www.businessinsider.com/lottery-winners-lost-everything-2017-8.
2. »José Mujica,« *Wikipedia*, accessed September 1, 2021, https://en.wikipedia.org/wiki/Jos%C3%A9_Mujica.
3. Vladimir Hernandez, "Jose Mujica: The world's 'poorest' president," *BBC*, accessed September 1, 2021, https://www.bbc.com/news/magazine-20243493.

58. Thought leaders think

1. Steve Denning, "Why did IBM survive?" *Forbes*, accessed September 1, 2021, https://www.forbes.com/sites/stevedenning/2011/07/10/why-did-ibm-survive/.
2. "André Kostolany," *Wikipedia*, accessed September 1, 2021, https://en.wiki pedia.org/wiki/Andr%C3%A9_Kostolany

60. Thought leaders are constant learners

1. "Paul Dirac," *Wikipedia*, accessed September 1, 2021, https://en.wikipedia. org/wiki/Paul_Dirac

ABOUT THE AUTHOR

 Author Patrick Pissang worked as a sales engineer for MuleSoft from the early days to IPO and created innovative technical value-selling tools for his opportunities in the field. His philosophy is to lead the client with methods they don't expect—and therefore won't forget. He coaches customers while they run the proof of concept, and he uses domain-driven design to facilitate strategic discovery workshops. Patrick expanded his own original thinking into social media and now helps sales engineers build their brand. He is the lead trainer, founder, and CEO of Sales Hero GmbH, a company that specializes in training sales engineers.

He has already trained and coached sales engineering teams in companies like MuleSoft, Salesforce, Aiven, Workato, LeanIX, Kong, UKG, MSH, and Avast Business.

The other parts of his life are dedicated to his lovely family: his wife, two daughters, and two cats, and his professional fiction writing career under the pseudonym Lew Marschall.

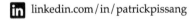 linkedin.com/in/patrickpissang

YOUR AI COMPANION!

AI will make parts of an SE's chores redundant. Who needs a human to explain technical features? For example, ChatGPT is more precise, available around the clock, and much more patient.

The interesting thing is that AI is replacing jobs and tasks considered irreplaceable. Remember artists and knowledge workers stating: "Never will technology be able to do what I do." And now, look at AI tools drawing every imaginable picture you want, prospecting business opportunities, and explaining complex software for six-year-olds.

So we Sales Engineers must learn to work with AI.

Decide the guide to educate yourself on navigating the AI storm and make it a companion instead of an enemy.

What you get

- 21 specific powerful prompts in seven categories
- Massive time saving for chores like desk research, discovery, qualification, objection handling, and more
- Designed for Sales Engineers from Sales Engineers
- Entirely tactical, ready to use, no bs prompts
- No hours-long training course needed
- No frustration testing out your prompt versions and exceeding quota on ChatGPT

presales.gumroad.com/l/sales-engineer-chatgpt-prompt-guide

Get your copy of the Sales Engineer's AI companion with a 25% reader's discount: TSSE-AI-25

ALSO BY SALESHERO & PATRICK PISSANG

More Books For Free Via The Sales Hero Newsletter

Sales Engineering Exposed

The Subtle Art of Sales Engineering

Courses

The Hero's Journey of the Sales Engineer

The Social Sales Engineer

The Three Diamonds

DFour – Strategic Discovery Using Domain-Driven Design

Coaching

No Competition

Interview Preparation

Or ask for your company's VIP bundle

https://saleshero.training

Made in United States
Troutdale, OR
01/02/2025

27513659R10139